ELK TALK

ELK TALK

Your Guide to Finding Elk, Calling Elk, and Hunting Elk
With a Rifle, Bow and Arrow or Camera

By DON LAUBACH and MARK HENCKEL

with introduction by Jim Zumbo

ISBN 10: 1-931832-90-0
ISBN 13: 978-1-931832-90-8
(Formerly ISBN 0-937959-22-7)

Library of Congress Catalog Card Number: 87-90834

Published by:
  Don Laubach
  Box 85
  Gardiner, MT 59030

Distributed by:
  RIVERBEND PUBLISHING
  P.O. Box 5833
  Helena, MT 59604
  1-866-787-2363
  www.riverbendpublishing.com

Printed in the United States of America.

  2 3 4 5 6 7 8 9 0 MG 15 14 13

Cover photo by Ron Shade
Illustrated by John Potter

Dedication

This book is dedicated to our wives,
Dee Laubach and Carol Henckel,

who have listened to more elk calling, heard more
elk stories, and tolerated our absence during
more elk seasons, than any two women
should ever be expected to endure
in long-standing marriages.

TABLE OF CONTENTS

ACKNOWLEDGEMENTS

Honest, dear, the typing is going to stop after I finish this very page. This page may be at the front of the book, but it's positively the last time you'll have to deal with authors for a long, long time. No more talking into tape recorders. No more late nights bent over a keyboard. But I've got to thank some people, before I send this book off to the printer.

There are the kids, of course, Wade, Kirk, Ryan, and Lori in Gardiner, and Andy and Matt in Park City. They heard more elk calling, and talk about elk, than anyone should have to bear. And they carried the burden of all sorts of things that their dad should have been doing, instead of writing a book.

Many thanks to Jim Zumbo, the excellent writer for Outdoor Life magazine out of Cody, Wyo., who not only offered his encouragement, but lent his writing talents to the introduction of Elk Talk. And thanks, too, to John Potter, of Billings, who added his creative talents in the form of the art work in this book.

There are hunting partners like Keith Wheat, Rod Churchwell, Doug Laubach, Mark Wright, Bill Hoppe, George Athas, Art Hobart, Curt Collins, Vince Yannone, Rob Seelye, and John Kremer, who have helped in learning more about elk during the season, and talked freely about their experiences when the season was done.

Gordon Eastman and Ralph Staton, of E.L.K., Inc., were invaluable in the development and production of my bull and cow calls. Ron Shade was more than generous with his photographic talents. And Wayne Schile, Dick Wesnick, and Warren Rogers, at the Billings Gazette, allowed more freedom for developing a writing talent than most bosses would ever consider.

There was Terry Lonner, of the Montana Department of Fish, Wildlife, and Parks, and Richard Mackie, wildlife professor at Montana State University, who helped in providing facts and figures on elk. Their unselfish efforts over the years, and all the work done by professional wildlife managers in the Northern Rockies, are what is keeping our elk herds alive and well.

And, finally, there were the proofreaders of this book, like Ralph Saunders, wives Dee Laubach and Carol Henckel, and the folks at Falcon Press who helped keep tired typing fingers from making too many typos.

Without the help and encouragement of all of them, Elk Talk would never have become a reality.

■

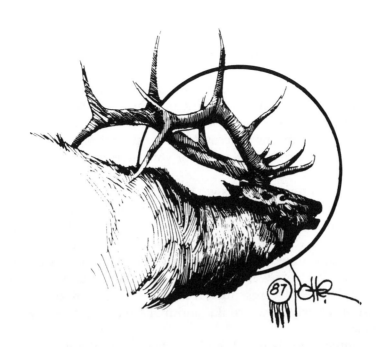

FOREWORD

When you've got two elk hunters writing a book about elk hunting, you've got yourself a basic problem.

For one thing, how do you write one book together, and yet live your separate hunting lives. When you use the word "I," who exactly is the "I?" When you describe someone as "a good friend," whose friend is it? You could, of course, create a character for yourself, something of a "Don-Mark." But hyphens are tough on the typing fingers. And when you've got elk hunters who are more comfortable fingering bowstrings and triggers than a typewriter keyboard, you run the constant risk of having it come out wrong. We tried it. And "Den-Mark," is a long way from the elk country of the Northern Rockies.

To make things easier on you, the reader, we just went with "I." "I" is Don. "I" is Mark. "We" is Don and Mark. And "my good friend" is just a good friend of one author that the other author hasn't met yet.

We, or is it I, used the names of these good friends often throughout this book. It's not that we are trying to name-drop. It's that the concepts of elk talk, and speaking the animals' own language in all seasons, is so new and revolutionary that there had to be someone to vouch for it. We sprinkled the book liberally with stories of our elk hunts and theirs'. This is not to pass down our hunting experiences to posterity. It's our hope, instead, that you can learn from our successes and misfortunes, and, in the process, be a little better prepared for your own experiences with elk.

Most of the hunting friends we talk about, are from cities and towns in Montana, which are duly identified. That's simply because we hail from here. The elk talk itself, however, has proved to work just as well in other elk states and provinces.

Elk talk is a universal language. And Elk Talk discusses the lifestyles of what we feel is the most magnificent animal in the Northern Rockies. In presenting it to you, we decided to present Elk Talk as clearly as we could, and make reading it as easy as possible.

The simple truth is that I, and we, hope you like it.

Don Laubach
Gardiner, Mont.

Mark Henckel
Park City, Mont.

■

INTRODUCTION

by Jim Zumbo

Of all the animals we hunt in North America, elk are by far the toughest. The big animals live in a rugged, vast mountainous region, and statistics show that it takes the average hunter five years to kill an elk.

When someone like Don Laubach comes along, people sit up and listen. Don takes an elk every year the hard way. He uses archery equipment, and hunts elk in September when the hills are alive with elk voices.

Besides being a skilled hunter, Don is a highly accomplished archer, and has a roomfull of trophies to prove it. His awards include state titles as well as those from national competition.

Born in Big Timber, Montana, Don started hunting elk as a youngster. Later, as a resident of Gardiner, Montana, Don continued his hunting in a region which I consider to be the ''elk capital of the world.''

As a Gardiner resident, Don lives with elk year-round. The animals stroll along the streets in the winter, and can be seen every day of the year, either within the city limits, on the hilly slopes around Gardiner, or within Yellowstone Park which borders the town. A crabapple tree in Don's front yard is a favorite feeding spot for wandering bulls.

Don observed elk closely, and learned their peculiar habits. Using that knowledge, he became a consistently successful hunter.

A couple years ago, Don realized that the standard technique of using a bugle call to attract elk could be improved upon. He knew that all elk were vocal, and began experimenting with cow calls. In 1985, he designed a cow call, and passed prototypes around to friends for testing purposes. I used it successfully, as did several outfitters and veteran elk hunters, and was sold on its effectiveness. The call opened a new dimension to elk hunting, and my story in *Outdoor Life:* "Elk Hunting's Newest Secret", introduced other hunters around the nation to the new call. Many of those hunters successfully called in elk, not only during the September breeding season, but during the late fall and winter as well.

Besides the cow call, Don also designed a new bugle call which is easy to use and extremely effective.

This book is an outstanding work that should be included in every elk hunter's library. Don shares his secrets and knowledge in a way that will improve any hunter's chances in elk country. You'll read about the real world of the elk, from the time they're born to the time they grow into giant bulls that all of us are looking for. You'll learn scores of tips and techniques from a pro who has done it all, seen it all, and isn't afraid to pass his secrets on to other hunters.

It's fitting that Mark Henckel should co-author this book with Don. As the outdoor editor for the *Billings Gazette,* Mark is an accomplished writer, and has a witty writing style that makes him a favorite among Montana's outdoorsmen.

Mark's book, "*A Hunter's Guide to Montana*", is a fine work that indicated his love the Big Sky State, as well as his skills in the outdoors.

Mark's superb editing and writing talents make this book a must for every person who intends to carry an elk tag in his or her pocket, no matter which state or Canadian province you intend to hunt. Whether you're an amateur or veteran elk hunter, this book will offer an enormous amount of information that can't help but make you a better elk hunter.

This book occupies a prime spot in my outdoor library, and I was proud to have been asked to write the introduction. Laubach and Henckel have turned out a superb piece of work that I'll refer to often. And I'm betting you will, too.

■

ELK TALK

Elk are many things to many hunters. They are magic. They are mystery. They are the ultimate trophy of the Northern Rockies.

Yet hunting strategies for them have changed very little over the past hundred years. We've been content to make their whistling calls in September. We search them out in the high mountain meadows of October. And we wait in ambush for the migratory herds that herald the coming of November's deep snows to the backcountry.

Hunters have complained that things just aren't like they used to be. With the growing popularity of the sport of elk hunting, the animals have changed. As more hunters have tried elk calling, the elk themselves have grown quiet. It's tougher than ever before to call in a bull. The elk have somehow gotten smarter than the elk hunters.

Yet, in truth, we've explored the language of elk very little over the past hundred years. We simply broke it down into bugles and barks, and left it at that. The bugles were made by bulls. The barks were made by cows. As for the calves, they were just sort of learning how to make bugles and barks for when they got older.

Most hunters have been too content with the situation. They

never really did their homework when it came to studying elk outside the archery and gun seasons. They never really learned that elk have a language all their own, which spans every month of the year, both sexes, and every age class. It's as commonly heard on the calving grounds of June as the winter range of January. It's part of the language of the peak of the rut in September, the time before the rut in August, and long after the rut is past in November. A hunter has to become fluent in this language, as well as the grunts, squeals, and bugles of breeding-time bulls, if he's going to consistently make his own successes in elk country.

The universal language we're speaking about is something we call cow talk. It's not that the cows are the only ones using it. Cows make the sound. Calves make the sound. Bulls make the sound. And even deer, antelope, and bears respond to it. The concept of this universal language is so new, that we really haven't explored all its possibilities. It seems to convey different meanings to different animals at different times. What we do know, however, is that if a hunter can speak the language, and know when to make those sounds with his elk call, he's halfway home when it comes to bagging his bull.

This sound we're talking about is elk talk, the language, and, in part, Elk Talk, the book.

But that only covers one aspect of Elk Talk. This book is a talk about elk, as well. Too few hunters seem to spend enough time in the field to get to know elk on an intimate basis. They pick up their information in bits and pieces over many hunting seasons.

Perhaps they live too far away to get into elk country on a regular basis at other times of the year. Maybe they're getting into the elk hunting game later in life, and need a quick primer on how to hunt them. Or, possibly, they have hunted them often and just require a little literary glue, to piece together their own experiences and have them make sense in regards to their past dealings with elk.

Whatever the reason, most hunters would be more successful if they knew a little more about the elk themselves, where they go, and what they do when they get there. These hunters rarely get the chance to see the calves being born. They understand very little about how bull bunches and cow clans live their segregated lives. And they don't realize that the heirarchy of the bulls dictates that each age class conforms to certain roles and will react to the hunter differently.

Bulls, cows and calves have a language all their own spoken in all seasons. Mark Henckel photo.

As a result, these hunters' success in finding and calling in elk, is often as limited as their understanding of that elk language. Because they didn't know the forces at work in an elk herd, their hunting too often was done in hit-and-miss fashion. In some years, they got into the elk. In other years, they didn't. And they never really knew the reasons why they did or didn't score, except that sometimes, luck smiled on them.

It takes more than luck, however, to be able to count on getting an elk on a regular basis. A hunter instead, should concentrate on controlling as many variables as he can. He should know where the elk are in all seasons, and why they are there. He should know their feeding tendencies, and how weather conditions play a role in moving elk. He should know his hunting country on an intimate basis, and in what parts of it the elk are going to be hiding. And, finally, he should know how to talk to the elk, and use their language to his advantage.

For an elk hunter to truly appreciate what he's going after in the high country, he should also know a little about the lifestyle of the animal. Even if he doesn't shoot a calf, he should know about the fragile beginnings of tomorrow's herd bulls and lead cows. If shooting a spike is or isn't fulfilling to him, he should still know about these babes of the woods which are out on their own for the first time in their lives. And if, in fact, he does come home with a herd bull in the back of his pickup truck, he should appreciate the years of apprenticeship that animal went through, the rarity of that trophy-class elk, and the forces that keep him in constant peril for his life throughout much of the year.

Elk Talk is very much a book on making bull talk and cow talk. It is a book on calling in elk. But the ability to call is only part of what this book is all about. And, it's only part of what hunters need to know about elk.

If the hunter can't find bulls, cows, and calves in the first place, the most beautiful calls in the world won't get him an elk. If the hunter doesn't appreciate the elk he has just taken, for all it has gone through in life, he has no business killing it. And if the hunter doesn't know the forces of man and beast at work in the elk world, he's not going to understand what's going on around him.

It's only by understanding both the talk about elk and the elk talk itself, that a hunter is going to make his own successes when the archery and gun seasons arrive. And, in the process, this

By learning where elk go in all seasons, hunters can make their own success. Ron Shade photo.

knowledge will help that hunter find the magic of elk talk that awaits him, in the high country that these magnificent animals call home.

■

CALF TALK

To understand where we're going, it's best to look at where we've been. So it goes with elk. Those magnificent six-point bulls, with the heavy, wide racks, didn't get that way instantly. And, for that matter, they didn't get that way by accident.

To understand the big bulls, understand the small calves first. The big bulls first found their voices and the meaning of their elk language in the first days after birth. They learned their calf talk in the nursery groups of summer. And they learned to communicate with the cows, spikes, and raghorns long before their bugling voices turned deep and menacing.

Just as their verbal skills grew, so, too, did their knowledge of the mountain world around them. In the high country summer, they learned of the trails from feeding to bedding areas. The migration routes became imbedded in their brains. And they learned the separate and unequal lifestyles of the older bulls and cows during the months of summer.

A hunter should also understand that the big bulls are survivors of many years in a harsh environment. Their antlers are the expression of that survival. The heavy, wide racks of the herd bulls are the prize for living a long life. The freak antlers are the chronicle of troubles along the way.

All these things are summer concerns of the elk. They tell a tale of lifestyles and tendencies among big bulls, cows, and calves just beginning their life. But, in the process, they build a base of knowledge for the hunter who chases elk in autumn. And it gives him an insight into the creatures he chases that just might make the difference in success and failure once the hunting season is here.

New Life and New Sounds

Elk life begins in a world of warm sun, wildflowers, lush grasses, and pesky mosquitoes. There is cool dew in the mornings, booming thunderheads in the afternoons, and the howl of coyotes after the sun goes down.

It's a harsh world, yet a sweet one, too, for the elk calves that greet their new lives in late May and early June. These calves, which will carry their heavy antlers proudly or bear young of their own in the years to come, enter life as solitary souls knowing only the warm lick of their mother's tongue and the sudden chill of hard ground.

But their imprinting into an elk world comes quickly. It was some years ago when I witnessed the birthing process and learned just how quickly and completely mother and calf play out their roles of survival. As soon as the calf was dropped, the cow began working with its tongue to clean its offspring's coat. Then the cow continued to lick the blood off everything in the area to remove the tell-tale scent of birth before predators could get a whiff.

The whole cleaning process took only about fifteen minutes and by the time it was done, the calf was already trying to get up on its feet. When it did gain its legs, the calf moved in on the cow instantly to feed without any urging or instruction. Its growth and initiation into the elk world had begun.

The peak of elk calving comes on about June 1, eight-and-a-half months after the breeding season of September, according to Terry Lonner, research biologist for the Department of Fish, Wildlife and Parks in Bozeman. "Most cows give birth to single calves and about eighty percent of them are born between May 15 and June 15," he said. "There aren't that many born in May, but they really pump them out from early June to mid-June."

The prime calving areas are away from the high mountain

The prime calving areas are away from the high mountain meadows and dark timber. Michael Sample photo.

meadows and dark timber that most people associate with elk. Calving areas tend to be in more wide-open areas and sagebrush becomes an ally of the cows and calves at this time of year. Cows will hide their calves amid the sagebrush in their first days of life, often using sun-bathed south-facing slopes to keep the calves warm during daylight hours. During that time, as the calves lay motionless in the safety of the sage, the cows will move off to feed. "Those cows will stash their calves and go about their business from four to eight hours," Lonner said. "While they're grazing and doing their thing, they can cruise several miles, but most of the time they'll be within a mile radius of their calves."

Lonner, who has studied elk calf mortality in the Gravelly and Snowcrest Ranges of Montana, said the wide-open areas have evolved as the places that provide the most security for the young calves. The tight ground cover of dense sage provides better concealment for the calves than the open understory of timbered areas. As a result, he has found that more calves are lost due to abandonment in the first days of life than to predators.

Growth and mobility come quickly for the newborn calves. It must if they're to survive. From a birth weight of twenty-five to thirty-five pounds, they will thrive on mother's milk and lush forage to reach weights of two-hundred pounds or more by the onset of winter. From wobbly steps on that first day of life, they will be ready to trail after their mothers for many miles each day when the time comes to head for the high country in July.

The first six weeks of life become critical for gaining weight and building this mobility. The vehicle that takes them there is the formation of nursery groups.

"After the first week of life, the cows and calves will start running in those nursery groups," Lonner said. "They start to form in mid-June and they're primarily for security reasons. That's the big plus. There is a lot of babysitting that goes on. The cows that are barren or lost a calf become aunts. Some mothers will watch them, too, while others move off to feed. We've seen these nursery groups with up to five-hundred cows and calves together. They'll run like that for a month, from mid-June to mid-July. Then they break up toward the end of July."

While calves have some voice at birth and cows will communicate with calling and barking throughout the period, it's likely that this nursing group time is when the young really

Nursery groups form in mid-June and may number five hundred cows and calves. Michael Sample photo.

discover their voices. Like children at play, the calves talk readily. And like human mothers, the cows answer back.

"There is a lot of social involvement and activity during that time," Lonner said. "There's a tremendous amount of talking by the elk. That's going on all the time, especially if there's danger. That's when the talking really starts. And it's done by every segment of the group, cows, calves, and young bulls. We've heard bulls bugling among those nursery groups.

"In the last 15 years, I've heard a bull bugle in every month of the year," he added. "They're always somewhat sexually active. It's just that this activity reaches a peak in autumn. And we've had reports of calves being dropped in October and November. Two guys from Butte I know came across a calf that was still steaming in early November. We've had cows near term in the Missouri Breaks in November. The cows get off on cycle and if they get off on cycle, they'll conceive in April and the calf will be dropped in fall. That's the exception, of course, but it can and does happen."

The main reason for the evolution of mid-summer nursery groups is undoubtedly security. But it's hard to imagine that the socialization process of the calves and making them accustomed

Calf Talk ■

to herd life doesn't come into play as well. Certainly that herd life helps contribute to survival through the nursery group period.

"At one time, the predators were wolves and bears and even coyotes. That's what set it in motion in the last 10,000 years. The bears are still out there. And you can't exclude man," he said. "The predators can't get to them when they're out in the open. It's pretty tough for a bear to slink through the sagebrush. The elk can see miles and miles around them."

If there's something that's surprising in these nursery groups, it's that the calves don't get lost in them. With so many cows and so many calves, the bonds of mother and young are still strong enough and so well imprinted that each mother knows its own and is able to find them and nurture them. No doubt smell comes into play in making the proper identification, but voice is another sure bet according to Lonner.

"How a calf tells its mother by verbalization is still a mystery, but we know they do it," he said. "It's something we don't have a lot of information on but I think they recognize each other's voices and physical characteristics like we do among humans. It has always amazed me that they could know each other individually when to us, all elk look pretty much the same. But when you get into a cow-calf group and disturb them and they run helter-skelter, within minutes, the calves are running with their mothers."

By mid-July when the hot summer sun begins to bake the sagebrush areas where cows have dropped their calves and nursery groups have gathered, the time arrives for those big nursery groups to break up. The calves are big enough and mobile enough to travel by that time. And the snow has receded in the high country, leaving parks and meadows of lush grass in its wake.

The day has arrived to introduce the calves to the mountain summering areas where they'll stay until the first frosts of autumn move them once more. Elk voices will be lost from the lowlands for a time as cow, calf and bull sounds resound through the high country once more.

Head for the High Ground

Elk calves have little time to bask in the warmth of the sagebrush summer. For these newest members of the elk family, safety,

New antlers are sprouting while old coats are shed in the early summer. Michael Sample photo.

security, and growth means heading for the high country when still very young.

New legs are tested early and when the calves are barely a month old, they will follow their mothers on paths that will lead them far into the mountains.

Terry Lonner, research biologist with the Montana Department of Fish, Wildlife and Parks at Bozeman, followed elk calves carrying radio transmitter collars and found their movements nothing short of remarkable.

"It's sort of like a hand with the bulk of the elk in the palm in the spring. And then you've got all these fingers going out where those animals go to and come back from," he said. "Some of those calves will have moved forty miles by the time they're a little over a month old and have climbed a couple or three thousand feet in elevation.

"It's about the same thing that happens with mule deer in the mountains. You've got the hub of the wheel and the spokes going out, except that with elk, the scale is three times that of deer."

At times, that migration to the high country may take these elk through several mountain ranges before they find the traditional use areas that the cows call home during the warm months of the year. Other times, the migration may simply take them to another part of the same range or even a different part of the same drainage.

Put in its simplest terms, and providing the best illustration of this movement, is a basin seven miles long and three miles wide which has been the home for a herd of four-hundred to five-hundred elk over the years. Each year, these elk drop their calves down low and then follow the receding snowline into the far reaches of the basin, working their way up timbered slopes until they reach the high divides which are marked by big grassy slopes.

Fueled by the hot summer sun, the fresh moisture of snowmelt, and ample amounts of ground water, those high slopes are covered with lush green grass at the height of summer. But the new grass of the post-snowmelt period isn't the only attraction for elk there. It's the sustained growth of vegetation provided by creeks and springs that creates the amount of feed needed to fuel growing elk.

Often, these springs and creeks of the high country produce water that's never seen in the valleys below. The springs may seep from the ground and flow only a few yards before going underground again. The creeks, too, may filter back through the layers of rock and earth or, if they do stretch toward the valley floor, may be diverted for irrigation uses. As a result, what may seem like nothing more than a trickle in the lowlands could signal a significant water source up above. Or, a patch of green spotted on a high slope could mark a viable spring that a band of elk will build their daily activities around.

Most of the high basins in the Rocky Mountains will have these water sources and the elk will move toward them as the summer sun bakes the low country where calves were born and the warm season began. There will be other features as well, that fit into the daily routine of an elk's life which are worth exploring for the person who hopes to snap an elk picture with his camera today, wants to bugle in a bull for his bow and arrow in September, or seeks to stalk the big bulls when the first snows dust the mountains.

The way to accomplish this is to work out the mysteries of a basin like the one which those four-hundred to five-hundred elk call home. And the way to work out the mystery is to walk the same trails that the elk walk as they move from place to place. Those trails are much the same as our highways in more ways than the obvious one of immediate travel. They also tend to follow the path of least resistance when traversing the terrain. And,

Even with their sleek summer coats, elk seek out the cooler areas in the timber. Bob Zellar photo.

finally, they tell the story of elk use in different seasons as those uses change.

The size and makeup of the trails, in fact, will tell a great deal to a person who pays attention to them. Some trails are long and well-used travel corridors from one drainage to another. Others may be short and not as well-defined, which shrink and then disappear at each end in bedding and feeding areas.

In the basin's case, the trails led to all these things in addition to a pair of mineral licks. One of them was in the timber and was used more by deer than elk. The other was on a hillside and had a spring in it and was marked by game trails which fanned out in all directions. Both were used heavily, especially during the summer months.

Elk in the basin had other considerations, as well, which determined their use of specific areas. Bedding areas were critical and varied during the course of the summer as the environment around the elk changed. On the one hand, there were several areas of heavy dark timber on the higher slopes which were used during mid-summer. On the other, there were the open, windy ridgetops which came into play later.

Though these types of habitat are vastly different, they accomplished much the same purpose for the elk. To get an idea of what that might be, just picture yourself in two situations. In the first, you put on every piece of winter clothing that you have and try to stay cool in the hottest months of the year. In the other situation, take off all your clothes and stand in the middle of a fly and mosquito-infested swamp. Put the two together and you have a crystal ball of what an elk battles in the summertime of the Rockies.

Elk wear a thicker coat of hair in the cold months, which is shed in late spring. But even their smooth, sleek summer coat is thick and heavy enough that heat presents a constant problem for them during the summer. As a result, the dark timber provides the best shade to beat the hot sun of July. It's cooler in that timber and, to make things even better, the biting flies and mosquitoes are less active in cooler temperatures. As the mosquitoes and flies get worse in August, elk head for the windy ridgetops where the wind will finally drive the pesky insects away and provide a breath of cool fresh air for the animals.

The best of both worlds can sometimes be found where a willow-lined high country creek forms a small valley as it cascades toward the lowlands. The willows provide shade, the cold waters of the creek create a microclimate of cool air and that cool air, in turn, gradually slides down the mountain making a slight breeze. These areas will often hold elk throughout the warm months of the year and well into September by making life more comfortable for the animals. In addition, those areas grow grass that can be munched for a snack during any hour of the day.

But don't feel that finding these bedding areas is only going to provide a glimpse of summertime elk. Once the time of many flies ends with the first frost and the hunting seasons begin, the elk will return to their mid-summer bedding areas in the dark timber. And those open windswept ridges could create elk opportunities in the late season when deep snows make travel difficult elsewhere.

The important thing is to walk out the trails to find the places where elk go in all seasons. The summer is the time to do that walking and exploring of new country. Understand those game trails and you know the easiest travel routes through the mountains, you find the travel routes, and you identify the bedding and feeding areas.

But working the trails, and even plotting them on a topo map, reaps side benefits that go beyond the summer of exploring in another way. By knowing where the trails go and how they fit into the pattern, they become travel routes for the hunter himself in fall. When the grasses wither and the leaves become too noisy for quiet walking, the game trails offer the silent walking conditions the hunter needs to slip in on elk unnoticed. And, after a summer of walking those trails, a hunter should have a pretty good idea of just where those elk will hide.

Bull Bunches and Cow Clans

It's a little like the difference between the men's poker club and the ladies' sewing circle. The guys get together, eat and belch, then tell a few raunchy jokes. The ladies eat, exchange a little gossip, and keep an eye on the kids to make sure they don't get into too much trouble.

The ladies are definitely more refined and, as a result, they can hold their gatherings in the beautiful living room. But the men may spill beer and disgust the more genteel nature of anyone who sees them, so they're banished to the basement or garage for their less-wholesome activities.

And so it goes with elk in the summertime. Those boorish bulls are separated from the comely cows. They may intermingle a bit on the feeding grounds by night. The cows may even tolerate the spike and raghorn bulls to gather with them, perhaps to prevent them from picking up bad habits from the older bulls. But most of the time, when the world can see who is keeping whose company, the two groups definitely go their own ways.

It's a fact of elk life that in these separations, the cows come out the winner. Throughout the year, they choose the best areas in which to live. Those are the places with the best feed, the most water, and the most secure living conditions. It's only natural that they would choose it in the summer. That's the time when the cows have calves to nourish, raise, and protect. The cows need the extra nutrition that the prime feeding areas provide them, both to make milk for their calves and still get enough energy from the lush grass to add to their own stores of body fat.

The older bulls, on the other hand, choose the less suitable areas throughout the year. In the winter, they often stay higher in elevation and buck deeper snows than the cows, even though they could just as easily move lower on the winter ranges to more prime areas. In summer, they do the same thing, going to places which are less desirable and making the most of the food, water, and shelter that these areas provide.

No one really knows why, even when both bull bunches and cow clans inhabit the same drainages that they utilize different parts of it. There's certainly nothing keeping the two groups from getting together. And there's no indication that the cows physically run the older bulls off the prime areas. Most likely, it's just a matter of survival over time. The elk herds that worked out this system tended to use their available summer range, both the good and bad parts of it, more completely and survived because of it.

The bulls invariably pick the more rugged country within the drainage. They'll pick up what food they can from amid the steep, rocky slopes. And, with only themselves to support, they'll thrive on it. The older bulls will add weight quickly during the months of June, July, and August. It's really all the opportunity they have between the survival situation of the winter range and the rigors of the rut, times during which those fat reserves will be burned.

The cows and calves, too, need to make the most of the rich summer feed in the prime portions of the summer range. Their areas will more likely be found in the open sub-alpine meadows where the grass grows green and tall and offers the most nutrition. The demands of the calves will be heavy on the cows during the early weeks of summer and they'll need all they can get from that forage. The cows' milk production will be all that sustains the calves for the first month. After that, the calves will begin feeding on their own but the milk will continue to supplement their diet for a time. Then the cows must begin to worry about building their own fat stores, which will be needed to get themselves through the winter and provide for the new calves which will be growing inside of them during that time.

The bulls form bachelor bunches and stay away from the cows during the summer. Jim Hamilton photo.

Summer is also the time of movement among young elk. It's the time of year when young bulls decide to establish their own home ranges and young cows decide whether they'll adopt the home ranges of their mothers. In the case of both sexes, that decision is generally made as they begin their third year of life.

It's a sign of independence for the elk. As calves and yearlings, their lives parallel those of their mothers. The spikes and yearling cows are roughly comparable to early teenagers in humans, big enough to be on their own but still in need of the guidance that the herds provide. By the time they're two-year-olds, they're more like humans in their late teens or early twenties and are ready to strike out on their own.

Cows are more likely to use the same home ranges as their mothers. Many members of these cow groups are related and the young cows will travel the same migration paths and use the same summer and winter ranges as their mothers.

Bulls, on the other hand, are much more likely to wander. In the third June of their lives, they'll take off in search of home ranges of their own. That search may carry them up to a hundred miles before they stop. And the type of area they choose may be quite different than the one used by their mothers. By the following year, they usually will have a home range established that they'll use for the rest of their lives.

Those home ranges will include well-defined feeding and bedding areas among other things. And the daily routines of the elk will include travel between those key elements of life. Until a person hunts them and follows their tracks, however, he doesn't realize just how far apart those feeding and bedding areas can be.

Elk are long-legged and built to cruise easily through the mountain habitats they call home. It's nothing for elk to move several miles in the evening to a prime feeding area and retrace its steps the next morning to bed in the same spot. Mike Fillinger, of Helena, would hunt several miles back into the mountains for his early morning ambush. The elk themselves would feed in some low hay meadows on the edge of the mountains but he would set up just short of their bedding grounds on a high divide. When the elk arrived, they would still be moving along at a good pace after their climb, but they were so full after a night of feeding, some were winded and even had their tongues hanging out gasping for breath.

The travel routes from bedding to feeding areas and back are typically in the timber. Most often, elk will travel the distance of up to several miles in less than an hour. The situation will change a bit in the fall during hunting season. As elk are pressured, they often cut back the distances they travel and their feeding areas may be more secluded than the ones used in summer.

Hunters scouting their chosen areas during the summer should be aware of the differences in behavior of the elk in the different seasons. The older bulls will generally be found in smaller bunches off by themselves. The cows, calves, raghorns, and spikes will be together in larger groups. And the travel routes are apt to be longer than in the hunting season. But that doesn't mean the hunter can't use the summer to get to know his chosen target a little better.

Summer is the prime time to explore new country and learn travel routes that might produce in the first few days of the season. It can even give the hunter an opportunity to get to know elk on a little more intimate basis and perhaps come away with a picture or two as a memory of his scouting trips. With so many young calves in the population, and the cows being so protective of them, the sound of a calf call can bring elk in close enough for a good picture using even a camera with a short lens.

Cows and calves get the choicest pieces of range in the high mountain meadows. Michael Sample photo.

A logger from Oregon was on his lunch break when he decided to try out a new call and got a quick response to it. He heard the calls of a group of cows and had a calf still wearing spots come to within eight feet and look straight at him. The calls of the cows lured it away after a time, but the logger called again and brought the calf back to within twenty feet the second time.

George Athas, a Gardiner outfitter, found a cow that was babysitting several calves. Athas got as close as he could without the cow seeing him, ending up just over the ridgetop from the group. He let out a single calf call from there, but didn't hear any reply. Raising up to see if they responded, Athas was surprised to see the cow just three feet away, staring at him.

One word of warning about calling, however, even in the summer. While it gives a hunter a good chance to hear how his hours of practice have paid off, it's easy to overdo it. Spend too much time making too many calls in your hunting area and the elk just might figure you out and become call-shy because of it.

Rob Seelye, a hunting friend from Laurel, advised me once that, in his opinion, elk had long memories. He would pick other spots away from his hunting area to practice his calling. And even during the season, if he called in some elk with one type of call on one day, he'd switch calls the next day to give himself a little different sound in the elk woods.

Use the summer, instead, to learn about your hunting area and learn it well. Go in quietly, stalk the trails, learn the places the elk use, discover their travel routes, identify the wallows, licks, and areas with rubs, and then get out and rest the area until the hunting season.

But along the way, you might do a little calling and pick up a priceless photo in return. You might hear the cows spreading a little gossip or scolding a calf. And you just might get a look at the old bulls' poker club and know what you're aiming for when the hunting season arrives.

The Rise and Fall of Antlers

Rightly or wrongly, antlers have always been the measure of elk hunting success. Drive through any town in elk country during hunting season with a big six-point bull sticking out of the back of your pickup truck and all eyes will turn. Try the same trick

Antler growth becomes a measure of heredity, nutrition, and individual history. Jim Hamilton photo.

with a spike bull, raghorn or even the biggest of cows and the sidelong glances will tell you that it's just another elk.

The reason for this, of course, is that a true trophy head is a rarity that deserves special attention. But what that small-town elk audience doesn't realize is that antlers are a changeable thing. And, in truth, they may not be the reliable measure of hunting ability or animal longevity which people often feel them to be.

Those big antlers of autumn are affected by many factors that reach beyond the hunting season. They are a measure of age, of course. But they are also affected by genetics. They vary by the area you're hunting. They're boosted or torn down by the good times and bad in range conditions. And they could very well reflect specific incidents that took place in recent times or years past.

Physiologically, the process of antler building is fairly well understood. But it's those variables which often determine whether a particular bull is going to have a great set of antlers, a good one or even a poor one in any given year.

The antler-building itself takes place in the spring and early summer just when the elk are taking advantage of the emergence of the best feed of the year. Their old antlers are dropped on the winter ranges beginning in late February. By mid-April, all but the odd bull have shed their headgear.

Even before the scab has disappeared from the dropping of those old antlers, new growth will begin in the form of fuzzy knobs on their heads. Antler growth from the pedicel, the bony base on the animals' skulls, can be impressive during the first few weeks as bulbous knobs of stretched velvet give promise of heavy antlers in the autumn ahead. It will take until late July before that growth will be completed and bulls will begin rubbing the velvet off their new set of antlers. But judging age or maturity from those antlers is a difficult, if not impossible, task.

It would be a far easier world if the points of elk antlers could be counted like rings on a tree stump or the growth lines on a bighorn sheep. Unfortunately, even just in the state of Montana, six-point bulls from Gardiner, the Missouri Breaks and the Gravelly Range could represent three distinctly different age groups. Antler growth is considered good in all three areas, but some are better than others.

Richard Mackie, wildlife professor at Montana State University, said antler growth was, for the most part, a mixture of three things,

The antlers grow inside a velvet sheath that is usually shed during early August. Ron Shade photo.

age, genetics and forage. "Age is one thing you can't get away from. It takes an old buck or bull to be a big one but the rate at which bigness is obtained can be influenced by other things," he said.

"It can be affected by genetics. You get a certain size and configuration of antlers that is in a population of a specific area." Using mule deer as an example, he said that even the biggest bucks of Montana's Missouri Breaks, an area he has studied for over twenty years, could never match the antler spread of those deer coming out of Colorado and Utah. But the good Breaks bucks all have a readily-distinguishable high, heavy, four-point rack that is their genetic heritage.

"When we flew the Missouri Breaks and looked at the elk, it was nothing to see six-points, some seven-by-sevens and even eight-by-eights. Five-points were rare. They were the raghorns. And we saw a lot of two and three-points among the yearlings," Mackie said. "In contrast, you look at elk in the Gravellies and after three-and-a-half years and even four-and-a-half, you'd have raggy five-points and five-by-sixes. How much that had to do with genetics and how much that had to do with forage conditions, I don't know. But you did get wide differences.

"Perhaps the greatest contributing factor to antler growth is

Calf Talk ■

forage. Forage is the single most-important thing affecting antler growth in a population," Mackie said. "I have heard references to mineral composition having some influence, but forage quality and abundance would be far more important. Experimentally, it's been widely shown that if you put an animal on good forage, you get a good thing going. If they don't have it, their antlers lose size and they may never recover that loss even when they get back on good forage."

Certainly, that good feed is necessary during the first few weeks of growth on the winter range in spring and when the bulls return to the high country to spend the months of early summer. But what many don't realize is that it's important the rest of the year as well.

Bulls need good summer range to go into the breeding season of September with ample fat reserves. They need to come out of the breeding season in good condition to survive on the winter range. And if they aren't in good condition coming off the winter range, they won't have the vitality to produce a good set of antlers for the coming year. In that way, it's easy to see how antlers can vary from year to year based on the amount and quality of forage available. Given a drought summer, antler growth will be retarded that fall and most likely the following one, also. Given several years of ample water and feed, antler growth will be enhanced.

Injuries can also affect the way antlers develop, both in the long run and short run. In the short run, the cause and effect relationship can be easily explained. Antlers are very sensitive during the growth stage and if they're bumped or battered, deformed points or the absence of points will be the end result. As to whether that malformed or unbalanced set of antlers will persist in the years to come depends to a large extent on the amount and type of damage that is done.

Mackie saw a bull for several years in the Missouri Breaks, for example, that carried a good set of antlers except that one of them emerged from just above the eye socket. Whether it was the result of damage to the skull or a genetic deformity wasn't known except that this is where the pedicel formed on the elk.

Long-term antler deformity, on the other hand, whether in the form of freak points, odd sizes or palmations like a moose antler, is almost surely caused by some sort of damage to the testicles of the animal which alters the amount of testosterone produced to trigger antler development. Leaping fences can be one cause of the testicle injury. Protuding sticks, stumps or logs can also hurt bulls. Or, the bull can be hurt in sparring or fighting. But whatever the cause, antler development can be severely affected with damage which eliminates, interrupts or reduces the flow of testosterone. As a result, an injury to the right testicle causes deformities in the left antler and left testicle damage is reflected in the right antler.

In the event of complete castration, the bulls will be stag-like and though antlers will often grow, they may never shed the velvet sheaths during the course of the year. The lack of sex drive simply takes them out of the life pattern of rubbing the antlers clean before the rut.

All of these factors cloud the antler issue. Suffice it to say that for hunters, photographers or simply sight-seers who want to find a good bull, they should be looking for animals that are a minimum of three-and-a-half years old in good elk range of autumn and more likely animals in the four and five-year-old classes. For true trophy-class bulls, an animal really needs growth until about their seventh or eighth years.

During that time, a typical elk should grow from the normal spikes of a yearling through the raghorn stages of two and three years and on to the brush bull status of small five and six-point racks. But just as surely as a long-lived elk will rise through the ranks of its species to the stage of dominant herd bull, the lucky few which survive to truly old age will go through a decline in antler growth. That decline, caused by a gradual loss in vitality, is the hallmark of all bulls which reach senior citizen status.

One such old, old bull was taken while hunting with Mark Wright some years ago. We had headed to the mountains with backpacks in search of bighorn sheep toward the tail end of the regular season.

Hunting and hiking in deep snow, a bull elk was spotted feeding on the side of a high mountain basin. A long stalk resulted in a three-hundred-yard shot which downed the animal, but it wasn't until we took a closer look at the bull that we realized just how old that bull was. The body was huge. His teeth were well-worn. Only one of his ivories remained and little was left of it. And, based on the amount of fat reserves, the bull was so old he hadn't even participated in the breeding activities that fall.

Calf Talk ■

In addition to these other signs, his antler growth had regressed to a heavy, but small, six-point rack. The main beam itself was only thirty inches long and the spread was about the same with eyeguards that measured just six inches long. In terms of symmetry, the rack was beautiful but in miniature of what it would have been during the animal's prime.

Taking the bull ended the sheep hunt, of course, and it took two days before we returned with horses to pack the elk out. Even then, the size of the old bull was still amazing. Two men couldn't lift a half onto the pack saddle and it had to be lowered with a pulley onto the horse's back.

It's doubtful that this elk's antlers would have brought much more than a passing glance in a town where people were used to seeing truly big elk. Yet that bull had eluded countless hunters who sought to bring him down in many past seasons.

So, just as there's more than a spring and summer of good feed that goes into producing a good set of antlers come autumn, the antlers themselves don't always tell the tale when measuring the longevity of a particular bull. There are many factors at work in the rise and fall of elk antlers which only make the true trophy head that much more of a treasure.

■

SETTING THE STAGE

Elk hunters can relate to the peak of the rut. They see the big bulls hooking and chasing cows. They hear the throaty bugles. And they call in the bulls when the first hunting seasons of autumn are in full swing.

But to really understand elk, you have to know how they got there. You have to do your homework first and pick up the tidbits of knowledge that could spell the difference between success and failure.

It does a hunter no good if he can call with the best of them, but can't find the elk in the first place. A hunter has to know about the transition period when the summer herds of bulls and cows break up and start wandering the peaks and valleys of elk country.

He has to know the feeding tendencies of elk, how they affect their lives, and the clues they provide him to unraveling the travel routes to and from bedding areas.

The hunter can use information that rubs and wallows offer. Some of these places indicate only where elk have been. Others will tell him where elk are likely to be.

And there's the difference between sparring and fighting among bulls. Each fulfills a specific role in establishing a pecking order among bulls once the rut arrives. Each also can play a part in deciding which bulls are more likely to answer his call.

To be a successful elk hunter, a person has to understand bulls and cows both in and out of hunting season. Knowing where they came from will provide invaluable information for the hunter who wants to know where to find them once he has his gun or bow in hand and a tag in his pocket.

Getting Ready for the Rut

There's a time in elk country when it's prime for a change. The mornings in the high mountain meadows have a certain crispness to them. The setting sun brings a breath of chill to the air. And though the aspen leaves are still bright green in color and the insects sing their chorus on hot afternoons, the weeks of mid-August leave no doubt that the warmth of summer is soon to be a memory.

It's that chill in the evening and the cool winds of the early morning that signal the change in seasons that is soon to be upon us. And it's a feeling that spreads throughout the outdoor world of man and beast. Outdoorsmen, too, feel a quickening pulse as they read the signs of teal and pintails beginning to pull out of the prairie wetlands, young mountain grouse gaining flight and brown and brook trout starting to show their spawning colors.

Hunters break out rifles in this magic time which haven't been touched since the autumn before. They go to the archery range to practice with bows and arrows. And wives begin to wince and groan as they hear the squawks and squeals of elk hunters tooting on their bugles.

In the elk world, things are changing too. The soft sheaths of velvet are starting to come off now, to reveal newly-hardened white antlers on the bulls. Sleek summer coats are gaining bulk again, as more hair is being added for fall and winter. Cows are gaining weight rapidly. Calves are showing more independence. And the big breakup is about to begin.

Bull bunches and cow clans have spent the summer in relative seclusion. Each group has gone its own way in the high mountain drainages with very little to do with one another. But in setting the stage for the rut, the first mixing occurs. The bull and

Bulls begin working up wallows as the stage is set for the breeding season. Mark Henckel photo.

cow groups break up and elk begin traveling more through the mountains.

The exact mechanism at work in this breakup is a matter of conjecture. It could be the invasion of the bull groups into the herds of cows and calves that precipitates the splitting of the cow herds. It might be that the summer forage has started to play out after the elk have spent many weeks in the same areas, while new feeding opportunities like the mushrooms in the black timber are just becoming available to them. Or, it could just as easily be the natural tendency among the cows that the time of year has arrived to move to traditional rutting areas.

In any event, the big cow-calf herds dissolve into smaller groups that take a bull or two or more with them. At this time, it appears the cows are the ones that are leading the way. The bulls are simply followers. These new herds that are formed are likely to represent every segment of the elk population. Big bulls and small, cows, spikes, and calves will move in the pre-rut groups as they cover new ground in elk country.

If there is a difference in how these new herd groups are formed and who instigates their formation, it's that the big bulls have been around this block before. They know the stages of the season and the rut that lies ahead. And they know the physical demands of the breeding season and what it will take out of them as they try to keep their cows in line, chase off other bulls, and do the majority of the breeding. As a result, it appears they try to grab as many cows as they can and get their breeding bunches in order as quickly as possible. Even now, with the peak of the rut a month in the future, they seem to be more serious about the herd formation that is taking place.

By getting when the getting is good, it's much easier for the dominant herd bulls to align themselves with the bigger bunches of cows. The smaller bulls are likely to take the breakup of the summer herds less seriously, simply tagging along with the new groups. Their energies at getting cows will come later when the full rut arrives. But by then, the breeding bunches will generally be in place and these younger bulls will play satellite roles to the big herd masters.

This pre-rut period generally extends through the weeks of mid to late August. During this time, there will be other changes going on in the elk world as well. Antlers will be rubbed. Wallows will come into use. Voices will be tested. Sparring activity will increase. And there may be the first bonafide fights of the season between herd bulls that bump into each other.

But at the start, the bulls will be tracking, and trailing after the cows as they get the herds in order. This following phenomenon is one that most hunters don't understand very well. Many hunters feel that the bulls, and the big bulls in particular, are the ones that are running the show in the late summer and early fall. Watching bulls hook cows with their antlers in the full rut, they figure that the old herd masters are always in control.

That's not necessarily true. In the pre-rut and throughout most of the rest of the year, it's the lead cows that direct the activities of the herd. And even in the peak of the rut itself, the cows exert a great deal of influence over where the herds will wander.

That the bulls are followers has been hammered home time after time as I watched bulls in late August and the first days of the

Bull bunches and cow clans begin to break up as breeding herds start to form.
Ron Shade photo.

archery season in September. I'm convinced, for example, that cows produce some type of secretion on their trail. This marks their movements as they travel through elk country and provides a way for bulls to more easily find them.

The bulls can actually track cows that way and you'll find bulls with their noses to the ground sniffing out a trail in the same way a bird dog finds pheasants. Even veteran wildlife cinematographer Gordon Eastman, of Powell, Wyo., was skeptical of this tracking and trailing when I first told him about it. But there was a time when we were working together on some elk filming, when we saw a bull doing just that.

The bull was working his way through an open park in which a herd of cows had recently passed. The bull came in with his nose to the ground and followed their tracks exactly. When the cows had zigged, he zigged. When they zagged, he zagged. And

Setting the Stage ■

all the while, he kept his nose in their tracks, oblivious to everything but their scent, as he followed them up the mountainside.

Another time, I was hunting with Bill Hoppe, a Gardiner outfitter, during the first days of the Montana archery season when we came upon a herd of five cows. Four of those cows spotted us and spooked out of the country. But the fifth cow was separated from the group, wasn't as quick on her feet, and stayed there, looking for the source of the danger. After a while, she decided it was time to go after the herd but she wasn't sure of the exact path they followed.

She put her nose to the ground and began going in ever-increasing circles, just as a good bird dog will do when he's casting for a scent. When she found the other cows' trail, she followed it until she lost it again. Then she repeated the process, making those circles again, until she rediscovered the tracks.

Except the final time she lost it, her last circle brought her within fifteen yards of me. The cow was just too big. She was too close. She was too easy. I couldn't resist. So I took her with a clean shot through the lungs, my arrow rattling into brush on the slope below her. The cow didn't even know she had been hit and looked at the source of the noise in the brush below. She just walked away and fell over, making for an awfully easy elk kill, one that was close enough to the road that we could drive right to it and load her up.

But before you bemoan the fact I filled my tag with a cow rather than a bull that year, rest assured it was more than compensated for by the good eating that cow provided the following winter. A prime cow is invariably better eating than a bull, especially a bull that has run off all its fat during the rut. He goes into archery and gun hunting times of October and November in its poorest shape of the year and isn't nearly as good to the hunter at the dinner table.

The most important thing for the hunter to remember about this season of transition is that the elk have started to move from their summering areas to the places they're found in the rut. Their habits are changing and they're starting to do things and show up in places that hunters can use to their benefit, once the first hunting seasons arrive.

It's time for the serious hunter to think about where the elk go and scout his hunting area well. Some cows and bulls will still be in this transition stage when the season begins. It's a changing world in elk country as we get closer to the rut. And the better a hunter understands that changing world, the better his chances will be of taking an elk in the first days of the season.

Elk in the Timber

An old saying goes that you are what you eat. That's true of elk, too. But perhaps more importantly for the elk hunter, they are where they eat. And where they travel. And where they bed. In fact, the toughest thing about hunting elk is usually finding the elk in the first place.

The best elk caller in the world couldn't bring in a bull if there are no elk in the area. On the other hand, even mediocre callers can score regularly on elk, simply because they've found where the elk are hiding. That concept may sound simple enough on the face of it. But how many hunters do you know that spend weeks and weeks working on their calling techniques, but don't get into the field until opening day? And how many hunters do you know who have taken elk, yet openly admit they're not very good at calling them in.

The reason for this is that the successful hunters know where to call, in addition to having some degree of skill at how to call. And the former is undeniably more important than the latter.

One of the clues that can help a hunter find those elk is to locate their feeding source. Elk are both creatures of habit, and opportunists, when it comes to picking their feeding areas. And their diet may be far more variable than the common hunter's conception of grass in high country meadows.

One instance comes to mind of a herd of elk that located a field of hailed-out oats near the edge of the mountains. That oat field became their nightly feeding grounds for weeks until the rifle season moved them out of the area.

Another time, it was stacks of freshly-cut hay which attracted their attention. The elk would move several miles from the high ridges down into those hay meadows to feed off the stacks. Their bugles filled the lowland evenings. And seeing the bright green hay pawed off the yellowed stacks every morning we hunted there, was a dead giveaway of their presence in the fields the night before.

Setting the Stage ■

Search for the best feed available in an area and it will probably lead you to elk. Michael Sample photo.

Alfalfa fields are another favorite in the weeks of autumn. While other plants wither in the first frosts of the year, alfalfa stays green and elk capitalize on it, often traveling for miles to reach the only field of lush feed in the country.

While all of these things may pull in elk on occasion, and hunters should be on the lookout for them, they might get more mileage out of elk feeding tendencies that go on year after year. One of these is the search for palatable grass when the first snow of the season descends on the high country.

After a summer of grazing the mountain meadows, that first snow changes the landscape and alters their feeding habits. The sweet grass of summer changes with the snow and cold of that first blanket of white. Even when they can paw for it, it doesn't seem to taste good to them. This change in the grass makes the elk pull out of the high country.

The elk head for the bottomlands where the high mountain cold hasn't reached the grass yet. They'll feed on the green grass there for a time, until it, too, changes with the cold. Then, they head for the high country again. By this time, the grass up there has cured and provides their primary forage base throughout the rest of the autumn.

While their visit to the low country may last for only a short time, it can make a significant difference to the early fall hunter who heads for the high country only to find that the elk appear to have vanished. Low country hunters, on the other hand, may benefit from a sudden influx of elk around the time of the first snow.

While that shows the tendency of elk in autumn, perhaps the most interesting feeding habit and the one that has consistently produced in my hunting has been the elk's love of mushrooms. Mushrooms are probably the last thing a hunter would think of as prime elk food, but when they emerge in my hunting area, they act like a powerful magnet to the bulls, cows, and calves that live there.

The specific mushroom that seems to turn the elk on here is one with a smooth, white cap that emerges in the month of September. The elk literally search and graze for them in the timber whenever they can be found. They snip these mushrooms off below the ground level taking leaves and sticks and dirt with them. All they leave behind is a small indentation, about two inches in diameter, in the earth from their muzzle where the mushroom used to be. Poke a little further in the indentation and you'll find a half-inch thick stem which is all that remains.

The elk actually go into a fungi feeding frenzy when the mushrooms are out. They wander in all directions through the timber in search of them. And whole herds will spread out to cover the area more effectively.

One of the first times I saw the mushroom mania, it was hard to believe. I had moved into a patch of timber ahead of the elk so that they were feeding toward me. I dropped my headnet and went into a patch of brush to better hide myself from them. There were about forty head of elk, most of them cows, and about ten deer in the bunch.

I couldn't figure out what they were doing at first. They'd take a bite of something here first, then go over there and take a bite, then wander a different direction and take a bite, and maybe wander back to where they started and take a bite again. While I was watching those elk, the group of deer had moved in behind me, including a four-point buck. The buck was suspicious, but couldn't make out exactly what I was until he came to within fifteen yards away. He finally spooked, but even when he took the other deer with him, the commotion didn't scare the elk.

The elk were so engrossed in eating mushrooms that the bounding deer didn't even attract their attention. The elk started moving past me, some of them as close as thirty yards and most of them within sixty yards. After they had passed, I investigated the sites where they were feeding and found the remains of the mushrooms.

Another time, I was hunting with Rod Churchwell when we walked up on four cows that were feeding on mushrooms in the timber. It was a close encounter that never should have taken place. The mountains were in poor shape for stalking or walking with dry leaves, twigs, and weeds making it impossible to move quietly. But the elk were so intent on their mushrooms that they never paid any attention as we moved to within twenty yards. The only thing that saved the cows was a limb that reached out and grabbed Churchwell's arrow and deflected its path.

The mushroom mania that grips elk country in early autumn has changed my September hunting strategy quite a bit over the years. This mushroom feeding period can last three to four weeks, unless it's stopped by cold weather. And even then, once the

One of the elk delicacies in the timber is a bumper crop of autumn mushrooms. Bob Zellar photo.

weather warms up again, the mushrooms will reappear. When they're out, the elk will definitely head for the dark timber in search of them.

Of course, I'm for hunting in the timber anytime. Perhaps it's my years of bowhunting, and the close-range shooting this necessitates, that makes me this way, but I've always felt that the timber is the only place to concentrate your efforts. The reason is that this is where elk spend most of their time whether there are mushrooms to be found or not.

Elk do work out into the open parks in the mornings. They even reappear there in the evenings. But during the bulk of the day, they're somewhere in that timber. That's why even in non-mushroom situations, the feeding areas are only a starting point in finding elk. Once they leave those feeding areas, they'll move through the timber to bedding areas, which are often in even thicker timber. If you want to hunt more than the first and last few minutes of the day, you'll have to hunt the timber to get close enough to the elk for a shot.

If there's a method to success, it's to find the feeding areas that the elk are using and let them be your guide. If you can't ambush them there in the morning, look to their travel routes to the bedding areas. If you can't find the travel routes, locate the bedding grounds themselves and look for logical paths in between. That way, you'll know where to find the elk at any hour of the day and, as we said earlier, finding elk in the first place is perhaps the most important single thing about calling and taking elk.

Working in the hunter's favor in autumn is that the elk will very likely be vocal in their movements. Bulls will be bugling. Cows and calves will be talking. And given a still morning, the sound of their chatter can help you unravel the mysteries of the feeding areas, travel routes, and bedding grounds.

Each of these things are like the pieces of an elk puzzle, with timber as the one constant that pulls them together. As you put those pieces in place, you'll not only increase your chances of taking an elk. By knowing where they'll be at any particular time, you'll find a way to stretch the productive hours of your hunting day from dawn until dusk.

Wallows And Rubs

Bill Hoppe has seen many elk do many things. A lifelong resident of the Gardiner area and a well-known and respected outfitter there, he has watched elk in all seasons.

Hoppe has seen the newborn calves suckle their mothers in spring, witnessed the cows' life-and-death struggles with deep snow in winter, and studied the habits of big bulls and small from the earliest of archery seasons in autumn through the late migrations of mid-winter. There are, in fact, few phases of elk life that Hoppe hasn't seen.

But one of the rarest views of the elk around him came one day during the archery season of early September when he was able to actually watch a bull work off steam in the water and mud of a wallow. That mature bulls use wallows, came as no surprise. The first sightings of active elk wallows and trees rubbed bare of bark are the most visible signs that bulls are getting ready for the rut. Spend much time in elk country and you're bound to run into one, the other, or both.

But while hunters during the breeding season will, at times, witness a bull rubbing and polishing his antlers on a tree, it's rare indeed to spot one tearing up a wallow. In Hoppe's case, his glimpse at wallowing activity came as he hunted near the head of a creek in a high mountain basin. He had seen other elk that day but was on his way back to camp when this bull answered his bugle.

"He was a long ways away when I first heard him and I kept walking toward him and walking toward him," Hoppe recalled. "Everytime I'd bugle, he'd bugle back. When I got over on this hillside, it was real steep and I looked down below me. He was right down at the head of the spring."

The five-point bull that Hoppe spotted was in the wallow working off steam and covering himself with mud. It was a striking sight, and one that seems incongruous with the sleek-coated bulls that most people see throughout the rest of the year.

"When I first saw him, he was on his back," Hoppe said. "Just like a horse would lay down and roll, he was rolling in the mud on his back. Then I bugled and he got up on his hind legs and walked on his front knees sort of pushing himself along with his back legs. He was running his horns down in the mud and he'd shake his horns and the mud would just fly."

Hoppe was just two-hundred yards away when his bugling finally lured the bull out of the wallow. The bull climbed the slope toward him, went out of sight for a minute, then emerged at what Hoppe guessed was forty yards. The first arrow went over the top of the bull and the animal jumped. But a squealing call stopped him and using his thirty-yard pin, Hoppe delivered the fatal shot.

The bull, of course, was covered with mud. And seeing them with a fresh coating of mud or with the vestiges of hardened mud from an earlier go in the wallows is not uncommon during the last weeks of August or through the month of September. During that time, wallows are very much a part of daily life for the mature bulls.

Without the benefit of actually having an elk to interview on the subject, it comes down to a matter of conjecture as to why the bulls frequent the wallows. But theories on the subject point to several possible reasons.

The first, and most widespread among them, is that the wallows serve a cooling function for the bulls. Because the bulls are so physically active during the rut and they're so emotionally charged, their temperature is elevated as well and the wallows help cool them off. If there's a flaw in the theory, it's that cool, clean water would serve their purpose just as well and there are mountain creeks in most of the same areas where wallows are found.

Another theory behind wallowing is that the wallows serve to spread an individual bull's scent and impregnate that scent into its coat. Visit any wallow site and the scent of elk urine is unmistakable. They urinate in the mud, roll in it, and thus the wallow becomes both a place and a method to mark a bull's territory just as a male dog will leave his brand on trees, bushes, and, sometimes even fire hydrants to designate his turf. The wallow, then, is something like a bull's version of a high mountain fire hydrant.

A third theory is that the coating of mud somehow makes one bull look more imposing to other bulls. They work off steam by tearing up the earth around the wallow, coat themselves with mud, and, in the process, boost their egos and become more courageous by their show of strength. When they emerge from the wallows, their minds and bodies are hardened for the task ahead of battling other bulls and satisfying their harems of cows.

Elk will rub down saplings and small trees, leaving a legacy over a wide area. Ron Shade photo.

Most likely, however, the wallows do all these things for bulls and possibly fulfill a few more needs that man hasn't thought of. All man knows is that elk wallows are very much a part of rutting season for the bulls. That, of course, and the fact that elk wallows can be a great place to look for bulls just before and during the rut.

As to the wallows themselves, they generally fall into two types. One of them could be called a swamp wallow and is made in an open meadow or park where the ground is wet and soft. These wallows are usually used by many elk and grow to be quite large in size. Timber wallows, on the other hand, are smaller and tend to be used by fewer individual elk. Both kinds will attract elk in early fall but the timber wallow is more likely to be the hunter's friend. During daylight hours, the elk spend most of their time in the timber and the wallow there, in turn, is the best bet to hold elk during the time that the hunter can reach them.

One constant about wallows that hunters can use to their advantage is that bulls tend to use the same wallows year after year. As a result, thorough scouting and really learning an area well may do more than just help your hunting this season. It could pay dividends in years to come, as well. That doesn't mean, however, that new wallows might not appear. New wallows are pawed, hooked, thrashed, and rolled into existence each year by bulls. Most often, they're found by the hunter's nose as well as his eyes. Because the elk use them so hard and do urinate in the area, their pungent odor will perk up a hunter's nostrils and cause him to literally follow his nose right to the site.

To check if a wallow is being used, just look at the water in it. If the water is muddy, it has been visited recently by a bull. If it's clear, the bulls may not be in the immediate area that day. A check for recent tracks, however, could tell the hunter whether the wallow might produce for him later that day or in the days ahead.

The thing to remember is to believe in them. Wallows produce almost without regard to weather or time of season. And that holds true no matter what your pet theory of the reason for their use.

There was one time, for example, when it was so cold that there was snow on the ground and the wallow had frozen over by first light. Fresh mud was thrown far and wide on the snow. The water was still muddy beneath the ice. And a hunter who espoused the theory of bulls using them because they were overheated would

Elk wallows are used to cool the bulls, spread their scent, and make them feel tough. Don Laubach photo.

have a hard time proving it considering the local weather conditions.

Another time, Vince Yannone, of Helena, shot a bull in the rifle season that was caked with mud from one end of his body to the other. The time was late October, when all rutting activity really should have been over for nearly a month. Yet this bull had obviously been in a wallow quite recently. A hard one to explain, yet it did provide a problem to chew on while chewing on that bull at the dinner table in the winter that followed.

While wallows are physical attractions for elk, rubs are more of an indicator that bulls have been in the area in the past. They are not, however, guarantees that elk will be back today or tomorrow.

Rubs are caused by bulls working their antlers up and down on trees to the point they peel and wear off the bark. These rubs are easy to spot. Old rubs will scar trees with bare spots for years.

New rubs on pines will be running sap and elk hair will still be clinging to the tree. And saplings that are worked over will be torn up and broken as if someone took a hatchet to them.

Some feel that elk do this simply to rub the velvet off their newly-hardened antlers in the months of August and September. But that takes a far too simplistic view of the habit.

Like wallows, rubs probably accomplish many more things for the bulls as they get ready for the rut. They do remove the velvet. They stain and polish the antlers. They help bulls work off steam and work up courage. And it's likely that they also serve as another form of that high mountain fire hydrant where bulls leave their scent and mark their territory through urination or with a scent gland located near the eye.

One thing is certain. Rubs are one method of determining elk travel routes during the time before and during the rut. Brush bulls, those adolescents and young adults of the elk world, will rub down trees and tear up saplings at every opportunity at this time of year as they wander the mountains. As a result, there are many single rubs scattered along travel routes. And anywhere there is a concentration of elk, there will be many such rubs. Whether those brush bulls do it to impress the ladies who happen to be in the vicinity or out of sheer frustration for not being old enough to hold onto a harem of their own is anybody's guess. But their rubs are certainly there to be found all through the high country by rut's end.

Older bulls rub and polish their antlers, too, but the likelihood they do it as much goes against common logic. Those herd bulls spend so much time trying to hold their harems together and drive off other suitors that there probably isn't much time and energy left for them to make a lot of rubs once the rut starts in earnest.

As for spikes, they don't rub much at all. If they do, it's just to remove the last vestiges of velvet. Their sex drive probably isn't developed strongly enough in most instances to rub more. And some spikes even carry their velvet through the entire first year without ever rubbing it off.

Hunters can use those rubs to their advantage by looking for areas where they are concentrated. Those areas, where many old and new rubs are found together can mark places that are preferred by elk just before and during the rut. It's often indicative of a high elk use area. It's often on a north-facing slope in timber where elk will spend a portion of their early morning or late after-noon time. And it's often a strong clue that you're close to one of their bedding areas.

As a result, slopes where many old and new rubs are found can be good places to try calling for elk. The important thing here is to be able to judge the age of rubs and to realize that even if they were made yesterday that the elk might have moved on by today.

But just like wallows, rubs give a hunter an edge and a starting point. Both can tell a hunter whether or not elk have been using an area recently. Both are indicators that the rut is either ready to begin or has begun in the area you are hunting. And wallows and rubs mean one more thing to a hunter that's even more impor-tant. Together, they are that last sure sign that it's time to make calf talk, cow talk and bull talk because the elk are ready and willing to answer your call.

Sparring and Fighting

Like people, bull elk sometimes have these spats, little and big. They play, argue, tussle, and sometimes get violent with each other. They punch at each other with their hooves and the bulls use their massive antlers as lethal weapons.

Sometimes, these differences are all in fun. Sometimes, they get serious. And sometimes, they start serious and stay that way. What we're talking about here is sparring and fighting and there's a big difference between the two in the elk world.

Sparring is an almost continuous action by the bulls. It starts as soon as their antlers get hard in August and lasts until they're shed in spring. Even bulls with just a few points do it. They push and shove against each other for long periods of time, until one or the other of the sparring partners gets tired of it.

The real fighting is done by the big herd bulls and that action is pretty much restricted to the rut. It's quick, and violent, and sometimes fatal. These are the fights that we hear about in legend, with herd rights at stake and two monsters of the forest going head to head and antler to antler. In truth, they're much rarer than you'd imagine.

Big bulls rely on the bluff as much as the battle when it comes to establishing herd dominance. If their racks are heavier and their bodies bigger, the smaller bulls will almost always back down. It's folly for them to go up against that kind of bulk and weaponry.

Younger bulls will participate in sparring matches throughout the year.
Bob Zellar photo.

Most often, that's the way the confrontations end. But there are some true fights in the elk world.

Jim Hamilton, a wildlife photographer from Cody, Wyo., witnessed just such a fight while taking elk photos in Yellowstone National Park. Hamilton was following a lone bugling bull just before the peak of the rut. The bull was bugling constantly as he worked his way up a mile-long slope.

When he was nearly to the top, a second bull came down and faced him. The upper bull hadn't bugled much, but when his harem was threatened, he answered the challenge. Both bulls walked stiff-legged, parallel to one another, just as bighorn sheep do when they're spoiling for a fight. And when the time was right, they turned and made a short charge, crashing their antlers together in a violent blow.

In Hamilton's case, however, one of the bulls wasn't quite square to the other when they hit. Though the antlers of the two herd bulls were just about equal, the bigger-bodied bull came in at a slight angle. And when they struck, one of the brow tines on his antlers pierced the bull Hamilton had been following just above the nostril, cutting through into his mouth. The bigger bull moved off leaving his foe to mend a vicious wound, one that bled profusely. It forced the wounded bull to lie down for a half-hour. But when Hamilton checked on him later, the bull was up and chasing cows as if it never happened.

With the violence of these fights, they rarely last long unless the combatants are very evenly matched. When they do last, they invariably draw a crowd made up of other bulls in the area much the same way as schoolyard fisticuffs will attract the attention of other children. That tendency to draw a crowd has led some hunters to try their luck rattling antlers for bulls, much the same way as white-tailed deer hunters will rattle up bucks during the rut. These rattling elk hunters have had some success at the game, too.

Most often, however, the fights are of relatively short duration. The strength of the bulls and the potency of their weaponry dictate that injury can come quickly. The bulls strike down with their antlers bringing the fourth, or dagger point, into play. This, the longest of the antler points on an elk, is a vicious stiletto. In winter range situations, those dagger points have killed other elk instantly in sparring matches by piercing skulls or lungs. And if the dagger point doesn't work, the eyeguards, or brow tines, can do damage as they did with Hamilton's bull.

If the points don't do harm, often the physical strength combined with the heaviness of the beam of the antlers will get the job done. Ron Shade, another wildlife photographer from Gardiner, was watching two bulls fight when the right antler of one of the elk was broken off halfway up the main beam. It's not uncommon at all to take bulls with broken tines in fall. These are just as surely a sign of their battles, as any scars would be.

These fights are pretty much restricted to the peak of the rut, however, and for the biggest of the bulls. Frankly, they are probably the only ones who could survive it. And their battles are very likely the culmination of a lifetime of training for them.

It's the sparring of the younger bulls that forms the training and proving grounds for elk. It starts as shoving matches between the small brush bulls, when they feel secure in their herd groups. As they get older, they get a bit more serious and begin to establish a pecking order in the bull bunches.

This pushing and shoving may go on for quite a while and the bulls will even make their squealing cow sounds as they do it.

Cows, and sometimes bulls, will fight by rearing up and punching with their front hooves. Jim Hamilton photo.

I was watching just such a shoving match once when one of the bulls finally grew tired of it and took off, running at full speed to get away from the other one. Obviously, the running bull was the loser in the match and, as a result, fell below the other in terms of dominance.

This sparring activity begins just after the bulls' antlers harden and their velvet is shed. At this time of year, the bulls are still hanging together in their summer groups which may hold individuals of all ages, from the big herd masters on down to the brush bulls recently removed from the cow herds. As the sparring takes place, it's easy to see which elk among the group are more serious about it.

No one bothers the big herd bull. With his age, antlers, and body, a bluff is all he needs to show his position of strength. The youngest bulls are very likely just playing at their sparring and will push and shove for the fun of it. In between are the bulls ready to assume dominance once the old boy is gone. These bulls have very little time for the play of the youngsters, but know they don't have a chance at tackling the big guy. As a result, their sparring is somewhere in between the play of the young and the serious fights of the old. These are the bulls that are really attempting to prove themselves in the sparring matches and, in the process, are preparing themselves for the serious fights of the future.

That doesn't mean there can't be injuries and even deaths from sparring matches, especially when one of these in-between bulls is tackled by one younger and smaller than himself. There were two bulls sparring near the Gardiner River, one of which was obviously bigger than the other. They were shoving each other around when their horns apparently became locked and the older bull shoved the other off the river bank. The fall broke the neck of the younger bull and killed him before the older bull was able to pull his antlers free.

Aside from establishing a pecking order among the bulls, the sparring also serves a purpose when the rut arrives. Bulls that stay together know which among them is the toughest, the second-toughest, and on down the line. As a result, when the harems of cows are gathered for the breeding season, each bull knows which among them is capable of holding their cows and which are not. The games of bluff and keep-away are thus made easier when you know who's the toughest. A bigger bull can simply bluff a smaller one out of his cows. And the smaller bull knows which of the big bulls to stay away from if he's to keep his ladies in line until the breeding time arrives.

With that in mind, it's likely that the serious fighting among elk takes place when there are bulls of different groups that happen to meet. When the big, old bull of one group meets the big, old bull of another, that's when tempers will flare and the fighting will be in earnest. Blood may be shed. Antlers may be locked, shattered, or broken. And lives may even be lost before the fighting is done.

That's also the time when the sparring of the young bulls will come into play. If they learned their lessons well as a brush bull, added to their store of knowledge in the in-between years, and have the edge in antler mass and muscle, they'll win the big fight. And their prize will be the love of their ladies, when breeding time comes to the mountains of elk country in September, and to the victor goes the spoils.

■

COW TALK

Clear your mind of everything you've ever heard about calling in elk in the past. Just tuck it away for future reference. You'll need some of that old-time bugling later. For now, just sit back and be receptive to the new revolution in elk calling. And have faith, brethren, for we're talking about making elk magic.

While words like revolution, faith, and magic may seem like strong statements to be making about something as old as calling in an elk, the concept of cow talk is just that. In fact, the concept is only in its infancy as a widespread tool for hunting elk. And those few who have chanced upon it and been using it for a number of years have guarded their secret well.

This book and, specifically, this chapter are designed to bring cow talk out of the closet. In the light of day, it is making believers of even the most skeptical of hunters. It's working on bulls. It's working on cows. It's working on mule deer. It's working on black bears. It's working on antelope. It's even working on coyotes, mountain lions, and grizzly bears.

Cow talk is such a deadly force for the hunter that we frankly don't know where it will all end. At the time of this writing, it's only been in the testing phase for several years and in common usage for a single hunting season. But if the early reports are any indication of its future success, the concept will be as revolutionary to the hunting world as such things as gunpowder, the rifle scope, the compound bow, and the four-wheel drive.

Making Elk Magic

Hunters have been going about the business of calling in elk all wrong. They saw big bulls. They heard big bulls. They wanted big bulls. So they figured the only way to get a big bull was to imitate the sounds the big bulls were making.

Hunters ignored the calf sounds that the big bulls made when they were young and were accustomed to hearing since the day they were born. They ignored the cow sounds, too, even though those cow calls made up the bulk of the elk language throughout the year and the majority of the conversation between elk of all sexes.

Instead, they bugled, grunted, and tooted on elk whistles all through the high country autumn. And, they took some elk by using all those techniques. But what they found was that conditions had to be just right for that bugling, grunting, and tooting to work. There had to be a rut-crazed bull out in front of you, one so red-hot that he wasn't all that particular about the sound a hunter was making. At times like those, just about any bull talk would work. As a result, the only hunters who consistently scored on those bulls were the ones who had plenty of time and energy and luck to put into their hunts. They had to cover enough miles and blow enough chances at lukewarm bulls to find their red-hot victim. They had to be out in the high country for enough days that they hit the time and place where the peak of the rut was in full swing. Or, they had to be godawful lucky, and not a one of us was blessed with enough of that commodity to consistently take big bulls on an annual basis.

The problem with all this bull talk was that it was ineffective too much of the time. It was also much too precise in its execution. A hunter wasted too much of his season waiting for it to work or bemoaning the fact the peak of the rut had already passed. If only I had been at Rock Creek yesterday. If only the rut would heat up in Timber Creek tomorrow. If only we could be at the right place at the right time. Even then, if you just happened to

The language of cow talk is something elk understand from the day they're born. Michael Sample photo.

hit the peak of the rut where you just happened to be hunting, one sour note on the call and the bull spooked and the whole thing fell apart. That's called real elk hunting frustration in this neck of the woods.

What hunters needed was a little magic that wasn't so precise in its application and would work more of the time. They needed magic that would work in the pre-rut period, the peak of the rut, and after the rut. And, as long as they felt they were asking for the impossible, why limit the magic to the fall? Why not have it work during the spring, summer, and winter, too.

What they didn't know was that this magic was entirely within their grasp. It was right there in front of them in every season of the year, ringing in their ears while they strained to hear those beautiful big bull bugles. The magic was cow talk. But though every serious elk hunter had heard the sounds, few of them realized that the language of the cows and calves would or could be that effective in luring in elk of all persuasions. Some of them still don't believe it — until they try it.

Yet if you think about it a little bit, using cow and calf talk is

Imitating the call of a young elk is the most effective sound a hunter can make. Bob Zellar photo.

only logical. Elk are very much a communal animal. Almost from the day they're born, they understand the security of hanging together in herds. They spend every season of the year together in groups from the cow-calf nursery groups of summer, to the breeding bunches of fall, through the big herds on the winter range. Calves cling to the cows. Cows seek the company of other cows. Spike bulls are looking for any company they can get. Brush bulls are trying to get a cadre of cows of their own. And even big herd bulls in the rut aren't looking for other bulls. That's the last thing they want to see or hear. Those big bulls want cows, and the calves that bring cows with them, to add to their harems.

The cow and calf sounds we're talking about here are something of a mixture of a high-pitched chirp and a mewing sound. Calves and younger cows say it shorter and more high-pitched. Put it in type and it comes out ee-uh. As the cows get older, their call becomes a bit huskier and longer in duration. That, in type, would read as more like eee-ow. The beauty of the cow call, however, is that it isn't that critical in its execution. Listen to a big herd of elk and the range of noises that they make will be wide indeed.

Imitating that call has been done in several ways over the years. Vince Yannone, an elk hunter with a 17-year string of success from Helena, simply uses his throat, cupping his hands around his mouth to produce his cow sounds. He makes them on the inhale and has called in elk throughout his fall hunts.

Since the widespread adoption of the diaphragm turkey call as the be-all and end-all of the elk calling world, any number of hunters have used these to imitate cows and calves. But most of these hunters, too, have still concentrated their efforts at making bull bugles and grunts with them.

Given a little room for bias here, our favorite is the "Cow Talk" call produced by E.L.K., Inc. The reason is simple, we developed it and patented it, along with another call to make the traditional bull talk. It's easy to use and relies on a stretched latex band on a molded frame to produce the cow and calf sounds. At this time, it's the only outside-the-mouth, bite-and-blow cow call on the market.

But the way you make the call isn't important. Pick your own poison when it comes to the choice of call you buy. The important thing is to have faith in the sounds and make them. Used all alone, or in combination with bull talk, cow and calf sounds make magic in the elk woods.

The reason this call is so effective isn't really understood. Nor is the actual meaning of the calls. What we do know about the cow-calf sounds is that they start at a high pitch that is somehow reassuring to the animals. It's a pitch or frequency they don't relate to man which is a part of the elk's everyday language.

In truth, the cow and calf sounds appear to be very much the same. It's simply the age of the elk that makes them different. When young, their voice is higher in pitch and gets deeper as they mature. And the call isn't limited to cows and calves, either. Bulls use it as well. In fact, they very likely make the noise more often than the bugles and grunts which hunters associate with them. Those sounds are pretty much limited to the breeding season of autumn.

We're talking here about a language that we don't fully understand. We know what they say. We know what the elk do when they hear it. But as to the exact meaning of the cow call to them, it's about as clear as trying to understand someone telling us a story in Lithuanian. Not being Lithuanians ourselves, we just know that if we read certain Lithuanian words, we'd get a reaction from those of that national persuasion.

We have found that interpretations of the cow sounds seem to vary by season. In the summer, a cow-calf call will interest any calf or cow within earshot. In the pre-rut, they seem to signify a cow that might be looking to join a harem. During the rut, it's a cow that might be ready to breed. Just after the rut, it might signal a herd to join or a cow that hasn't been bred. And even during the late rifle hunts, it's a sound that seems to tell elk not to worry, that life here is more tranquil than it seems.

It's a come-on-over-and-see-me-sometime call. It's an ignore-your-nose-that's-really-not-a-man call. It's a forget-about-that-sour-note-on-the-bull-call call. And it's even a that-wasn't-really-a-rifle-bullet-whizzing-past-your-head call.

In short, the cow call is nothing short of unbelievable. It will do more things, at more times, under more situations, for more hunters, than any other sound a caller can make. There's no other way to describe the cow call than elk magic.

Calling Cow, Calling Bull

It was the best and worst of elk hunting situations. Russ Laubach and Kelly Tobin had the elk dead to rights. They were in the right position and ready to shoot. All they needed was to buy a precious fifteen minutes of time.

Laubach, one of the authors' nephews, and Tobin, his friend, were hunting in the rifle season just off Deckard Flat near Gardiner, a great place to ambush bulls after a night of feeding. The only problem was that the ambush was no secret to other hunters or the Montana Department of Fish, Wildlife and Parks. As a result and in the interest of safety, legal shooting time was set at 8 a.m., well after sunrise and the time the elk should have headed toward their bedding areas.

On this day, however, the bulls were still out on the flat, but so were some other hunters who rode out on horseback and spooked the elk 15 minutes before shooting time. Watching the elk move up the hill, Laubach and Tobin did all they could. They ducked in the timber ahead of the elk and tried to cut them off.

As the bulls came stepping fast up through the trees, Laubach pulled out his cow call and gave three blasts. At the first sound,

If elk answer your calling sequence, it's time to go straight to an answering routine. Ron Shade photo.

the bulls stopped and looked at him. By the second and third sounds, the bulls were feeding.

Over the next fifteen minutes, Laubach called every time the bulls started looking like they'd leave, a total of four more calls. But instead of leaving, they kept feeding toward him, right up to the 8 a.m. start of the hunting day. By 8:01, the hunting day was over and Laubach's and Tobin's bulls went down just fifty yards away. Not bad, calling in a bull in the third week of November, the fourth week of the rifle season, and late in the third month of hunting, if you throw in the early archery hunt.

But stopping a bull elk and holding him is only one way to use the cow call during the hunting season. Its applications really begin during the pre-rut period, extend through the height of the rut and on through the post-rut phases. There really aren't any times it doesn't work. And there aren't too many aspects of calling bulls and cows that can't be applied to the cow call.

One of the primary uses of cow talk, for example, is to locate elk and bring them in. It works for bulls or cows that way. The most simple locating sounds are made by blowing the cow call twice. After the first sound, wait five seconds, then blow it again. Often, if the elk are a long way off, that first call just gets their attention. It's the second call that finally elicits their response. If the elk are close, sometimes the first call will get the job done all by itself.

Because both bulls and cows will make the so-called cow sound, it often isn't clear what the hunter has in front of him. But if a hunter is working in timber, just getting that response is enough to tell him that elk can't be far off. Cow sounds usually don't carry more than a few hundred yards on the timbered mountain slopes. An elk is near. And it's time to begin a calling strategy to bring the animal closer.

Those strategies are just a bit different for calling in bulls and cows. Each sequence fulfills a different need of the animals a hunter is calling to. Each, however, relies on extensive use of the higher-pitched calf call. Why that higher-pitched call works better is a bit of a mystery, but it is true that there are more young animals than old in most healthy elk populations. The younger animals also tend to be more vocal. And, in truth, the differences in tone between a calf and young cow are slight.

As we said before, it's very likely that from calf to cow, the language itself is just the same, except that the voice of the elk has gotten deeper with maturity.

To talk to a cow, then, it's best to emphasize the higher-pitched calf or young cow sounds. That call is just about one second in duration compared to the longer and deeper two-second call of a more mature cow. A good, basic calling scheme for cows would be to go: calf call, wait five seconds, calf call, thirty to forty-five seconds, calf call, thirty to forty-five seconds, calf call, three seconds, calf call, three seconds, cow call, sixty to seventy-five seconds, cow call. If you don't get a response during that calling, stop and wait for ten to twenty minutes and move on.

If a cow answers while a hunter is in the midst of his calling sequence, it's time to go straight to an answering routine. For cows, that sequence would be: calf call, wait thirty seconds, calf call, thirty seconds, calf call. Until experimentation provides you with a reply for a cow that works better, this basic answer is a good one to use and build on.

The actual spacing between the initial sequence isn't that precise. The important thing to remember is to work into this or any other calling sequence for cows at a steady pace. If you cow talk too often and too quickly in succession, it has more of a tendency to alarm them and put them on the alert than to bring them closer.

"Cow Talk" Chart

CALLING A COW:

1st Minute					
10 sec.	20 sec.	30 sec.	40 sec.	50 sec.	60 sec.
c c			c		

2nd Minute					
10 sec.	20 sec.	30 sec.	40 sec.	50 sec.	60 sec.
c	c C				

3rd Minute					
10 sec.	20 sec.	30 sec.	40 sec.	50 sec.	60 sec.
	C				

Wait 10 to 20 minutes...try again or move to new calling location

LOCATING A BULL:

Method 1					
10 sec.	20 sec.	30 sec.	40 sec.	50 sec.	60 sec.
c c		c			

Method 2					
10 sec.	20 sec.	30 sec.	40 sec.	50 sec.	60 sec.
c c c					

Wait 10 to 20 minutes...try again or move to new calling location

ANSWERING A COW OR BULL:

1st Minute					
10 sec.	20 sec.	30 sec.	40 sec.	50 sec.	60 sec.
c		c			

Calling sequence can vary depending on answering animal

COVERING UP YOUR SOUNDS

1st Minute					
10 sec.	20 sec.	30 sec.	40 sec.	50 sec.	60 sec.
c					

CODE: (c) - 1 sec. in duration   (C) - 2 sec. in duration

Sometimes I will substitute a long call in place of a short cow call depending on the circumstances of the answering elk. In most of my calling sequences I prefer to use the short cow call. There will be times when you will vary your calling techniques from those recommended and it will then become your own pattern of calling.

It's been my experience, however, that even when I felt I called too much, the elk never bolted. They have walked away when agitated, but never ran off.

The theory behind the slower and steadier pace of calling for a cow is to soothe the animals, rather than excite them. What we want here is to give them the impression that all is fine here. The cows and calves are just having a little chat, how about you over there, and do you want to get together and exchange a little gossip on that nasty bull over in the next drainage?

Bulls require a little different strategy and a bit quicker pace to perk up their interest. The cow talk sequence to locate bulls is much shorter in duration. It's made up entirely of calf sounds and goes: calf call, wait five seconds, calf call, fifteen seconds, calf call. The ten to twenty-minute wait would be the same as the cows', to hear if a bull will answer or come in. From there, the calling strategy will depend on the time of year and if the animals are in the rut as to whether you mix squeals and bugles with your cow calls to bring in them in closer.

When making cow talk, one hint to help you turn yourself into a whole herd of cows and calves is to change your calling position. That can be done as easily as turning your head and blowing your call in a different direction to alter the sounds the elk receive. It gives the impression that there is more than one elk making the appropriate responses. Another way is to make the answering call, then move a little ways off, and do the answering call again. For elk that might be spooky, the slight change and the impression there are more elk answering them could be enough to make a difference in their response and bring them in more easily.

Don't get the impression from these sequences, however, that the calf call is the all-important and only tool of calling bulls and cows with cow talk. While these sequences do rely heavily on the higher-pitched sound, it comes down more to a matter of timing and the personalities of the elk themselves. The younger animals just tend to be more curious, talk more, and probably make up the bulk of the herd. They simply talk more. But the mature cow call is important, too, especially if a hunter is after a truly big bull. That mature cow call is deadly during the rut to bring in the old herd bulls, the ones that elk hunters spend their whole lives dreaming about.

But while it's easy for all of us to dream about those big bulls,

If the elk are a bit spooky, try to make your cow calls sound like a whole herd. Ron Shade photo.

we should point out here and now that there is no disgrace in taking a cow. In taking a lead cow, in fact, a hunter will have bagged an animal that's probably wiser than any bull that stalks the same mountains.

For those who don't know about lead cows, they're a fact of elk life without which entire herds have perished. They're an old cow and one with the experience and knowledge to lead the entire herd. In the old days when hunters were more willing to shoot as many elk as they could, then look for other hunters to tag them, the rule of thumb was to shoot the lead cow first. Without her, the rest of the herd would mill around and be easy targets for as long as a hunter cared to shoot.

One of my own experiences with a lead cow came some years back when I was calling to a young cow bedded in a nearby park. I was out in the open, hidden only in knee-high grass, when I started my cow calling sequence. The young cow was openly excited about it but as I watched her intently, there was a group of elk that came out of the timber that I didn't see.

It was the lead cow of that bunch that came in on a dead run toward me. She stopped at seventy yards in front of me, then came to fifty yards, but would come no closer. Yet she took command of the situation and held her ground when many a bull would have come closer and paid for it with their lives.

In many ways, the true story of cow talk is still being written. The concept is so new that the tales of success at bringing in elk are just starting to trickle in. But it's hard to dispute reports that have already been heard from throughout the West.

There was an Arkansas hunter, for example, whose group took one five-by-six and three six-by-six bulls from Idaho while making cow talk. A Colorado outfitter pulled three bulls within seventy-five yards at one time for his clients last season. Then there was the Wyoming hunter who was so excited at bringing in a six-point bull to ten yards in the first five minutes he made cow sounds, that he spooked it to twenty yards, where he missed a standing shot.

The only rule of thumb when using the cow call is to expect the unexpected. It's possible to stop elk and hold them like Russ Laubach did. It's possible to bring in a lead cow at a dead run. Or you can have an experience so frustrating that it's enough to make a person give up saddle horses for good.

Try sitting on a saddle horse sometime, making your cow sounds, and having ten elk come within twenty yards while your gear is securely packed away on the saddle. You're out there ready to hunt, but the only weapon you have is your cow call. It's sort of like being all dressed up, with no space to blow.

The Universal Language

A cow call is a cow call is a cow call, right? Not necessarily. The more we play around with cow calls, the more we're finding that the language is really much more than a way to talk to elk.

But before we go on, there should be some words of assurance and some honest communication between you and me. Just keep an open mind here as we talk about it, folks. Don't ask us to explain the things you read from here on. We don't understand them ourselves. All we know is that a lot of honest hunters keep telling us there's magic at work here for a lot of animal species.

Take the case of George Athas, an outfitter from Gardiner who helped out with prototype models of a cow call and has since become an unabashed disciple of the cow and calf sounds they make both in and out of elk hunting situations. In fact, one of

The sound of the calf call has stopped mule deer time after time for hunters. Ron Shade photo.

his main uses for the call is while hunting mule deer with his clients.

"I had some outstanding things happen while using the call," Athas said. "We had real good success at different times. We weren't really trying to call the deer in. We were just trying to stop the deer that we saw. But in the process of doing that, we actually did pull in other deer that we didn't see. We were making that calf sound and it accounted for five bucks this year.

"In two cases, we had a man shoot at a deer and miss and they were trying to get away and we stopped them and had them standing broadside. One man shot two times and the other shot three times, they ran off again and I stopped them again," Athas said.

He found the call to work exceptionally well for less-experienced shooters that hired him as a guide. Often, these hunters aren't as quick on the trigger as those who have spent more time with rifles in hand. Athas recalled one occasion when he spotted a huge buck for a woman he was guiding, when the cow call came into play.

"I had a lady hunting with me, when I stopped an exceptionally big buck five different times. We caught him out in the open. And he knew he was just out in the open naked. I stopped him there and it seemed to take her forever to get her gun and get out of the vehicle. Then she just aimed at it and the deer left. It just walked out. I stopped the deer again by using the cow call. It turned around and looked at us and she aimed at it and aimed at it and I thought she was going to shoot, but she didn't. So the deer walked off again. I stopped him again by making the call. I told her she had better start shooting because the deer wasn't going to do this forever. She finally did take one shot at him and she missed him and when she did, he ran. I stopped him one more time with the call and she never did get him, but it wasn't because of the call. I think she was shook up because he was such an exceptionally big buck. He was the biggest buck I've seen in the last fifteen years. It had eight points on each side. He was just exceptional and we never did see him again."

Athas said he concentrated on calf sounds when talking to mule deer. That one-second, high-pitched call seemed to stop them in their tracks. The notion of using high-pitched calls to stop deer for a shot isn't new. Frank Martin, of Lewistown, has long advocated using a sound similar to the call of a domestic goat or sheep to stop deer for a shot. He simply makes it with his throat while looking through the rifle scope, ready to shoot as soon as the animal stops. Martin and others have also found that predator calls would bring deer and antelope in to close range for a look while hunting for coyotes.

But the predator calls seemed to be more inconsistent than the cow call for stopping or bringing in deer. Sometimes, they liked the predator calls and did just what the hunter wanted. Other times, it seemed to act like a scaring device and the animals took off at a dead run.

More evidence that the cow call works as a mule deer call, as well, has turned up during elk hunting situations. But rarely do the hunters take note of it. Most often, they're concentrating so hard on the elk they're talking to that the deer turn into more of a sideshow and nuisance which could spook the elk. On one such occasion, I called in a five-point buck which would have been a prime candidate for a winter's worth of venison in the freezer had I been mule deer hunting at the time.

Mule deer aren't the only ones to fall victim to the sweet music of a cow call. An Idaho hunter, Terry Copper of Coeur d'Alene, worked his call for what could only rate as an unbelievable season of activity. That he called in four bull elk which were taken with the help of cow sounds isn't that surprising. But one day, he decided to experiment with it as a deer call. He managed to call in six cow elk and a bull with his sequence. After they took off, he moved a short distance and called again. This time, a big whitetail buck came into view and he shot him. The big whitetail scored 173 points and though Copper couldn't say for sure that the first sequence lured it into view, it's certain that the cow calling didn't scare it away, either. Another day, while making the cow sounds, Copper was sitting with his back to a tree with his rifle across his lap when he brought in a mountain lion. The lion came to within fifteen feet of him, where it laid down and looked the caller in the eye before deciding all was not right. The lion then moved away leaving Copper with yet another tale to tell about the cow call. Not bad for a single season with the cow call.

The calf sounds also have worked with black bears. Bowhunters during the early season, trying to call in elk, would get black bears coming in close enough for a shot. Coyote hunters have found

Hunters should be aware that the cow call has brought in black bears and grizzlies. Jim Hamilton photo.

the calf call to be at least as effective as calls being sold specifically for predators. And hunters have gotten responses, all of them unwanted, from grizzly bears as well.

One of the more interesting tales to come out of using the calf calls involved a Colorado hunter who ran into a problem with antelope. He was able to hunt on one side of the fence. On the other side of the fence, where he couldn't hunt, was a herd of thirty-five antelope. Using calf sounds, the hunter pulled the antelope through the fence and to within thirty-five yards to take his shot.

Once again, the cow and, especially, calf sounds seem to be just too good to be true. Don't ask us to explain why so many different species respond to it. But if pressed for our best-guess explanation of the phenomenon however we'd say it was probably because of the high-pitched sounds. For some reason, it's a noise that grabs their attention and invites them to investigate further. It's a call that seems to touch a nerve of every animal it reaches.

If you don't believe it works, that's fine. We found it a little hard to swallow, too, until we talked to people like Athas and Copper and remembered a few incidents of our own. Like the times the deer wandered in while we were talking to elk. Or the times the coyotes came in while we were talking to elk. Or the times the flocks of gray jays surrounded us when we were talking to elk.

Given a little time to experiment with it under conditions where we were specifically trying to call in these species, who knows how versatile those cow and calf sounds really could be? It's almost enough to make a guy give up elk hunting just to explore the possibilities. As I said, it's almost enough.

Learn to Listen

It takes a little retraining to be a good elk hunter. Through all our lives, we're taught to be visually-oriented. Sight is number one. All other senses come in a distant second.

To be a successful elk hunter, however, it's important to awaken all our senses. We have to train our eyes to see elk. But we need to train our noses to smell their tell-tale scent, too. And, perhaps most important of all, we have to use our ears to hear the things around us and to be able to interpret the things that our ears tell us.

A hunter should be able to identify and react to each sound he

Sometimes, a bedded bull will give just one call and a hunter has to be able to identify it. Mark Henckel photo.

hears in elk country. That sound could be a pine squirrel scolding an intruder. It may be a raven working on a fresh elk kill. Or it could be just a moving flock of gray jays, locally called camp robbers. That requires the hunter to become a bit of a naturalist and be aware of the different birds and animals that live in the mountains the elk call home. Yet that knowledge can reap dividends for him if he knows it when he needs it.

Even the absence of sound in the mountains can tell the hunter something. It tells him, in fact, that he's either not hunting in the right spot or isn't moving quietly enough through the timber. Elk seem to prefer to congregate in areas where there are also plenty of birds and small animals. That may be because of the type of habitat that the elk and other species like to call home, or it could be because the other animals provide an early warning system to danger for the elk. In any event, one seems to go with the other. And when there's complete silence, the hunter should be concerned about it. It's unnatural to have no squirrel chatter, no bird song and no insects chirping. That silence thus becomes a sign of danger for elk or a sign there probably are no elk in the area you're hunting.

The problem, then, becomes one of sorting out those bird, animal, and insect sounds. All hunters can easily recognize the bugle of a bull. But the normal cow and calf sounds tend to blend in easily with the calls of other birds and animals. The conversation between a flock of camp robbers, especially, can sound like a herd of elk and it may take a second or third call from the birds to positively identify it as coming from a feathered, rather than a furred, creature of the forest.

One thing to remember about these cow calls, and the call of the camp robbers too for that matter, are that they don't usually travel very far in the timber. About three-hundred yards is considered tops for birds or elk, though the filtering effect of the trees might make it difficult to tell exactly which direction the sound may be coming from.

Out in the open, the sounds travel much further. We did a test once on just how far that sound would carry out in the open. There were twenty-three bulls up on a hillside that we calculated, with an accurate range-finder, to be 1,660 yards away. We blew the cow call once, it took a moment for the sound to get there, and then all twenty-three heads lifted up in the air and turned in our direction. Once they heard the call, even that far away, it got an instant response.

The other elk sound that a hunter should be aware of is the bark. But this is one sound that a hunter really doesn't want to hear. The bark, which sounds amazingly close to the bark of a dog, is the elk's warning sound. Usually it's made after the elk see a hunter and identify him as a source of danger. And when they make the sound, it can be a sign for the whole herd to take off.

Back in my early days of elk calling, I can remember one of my first experiments with a grunt tube on a September bowhunting trip. It was rarely a pretty experiment. I had walked to within forty yards of a group of elk and had only to get around one more wide pine tree for a clear shot at a big cow. But halfway around that tree, one of the cows barked and the whole group started running away. With the tube in hand, I tried my best to grunt at them to stop. But that grunt sounded an awful lot like another bark and the whole herd simply kicked it into high gear instead, crashing through the timber for what seemed like a mile or more. That grunt tube always looked impressive enough stretched across my pack on those high country hunts, but I'm afraid it did more damage than good most of the times I put it to my mouth.

The sounds a hunter wants to hear and reproduce are the cow and calf sounds made by a herd of elk. That cow talk can help a hunter locate the elk and even tell him what the elk are doing at that time.

Elk seem to be most vocal in the early morning and late evening. That's when you're most likely to hear them. Cow talk can be heard in the afternoons, too, but because elk tend to be in the timber at that time of day, a hunter has to be very close to the herd to hear them. Also, that afternoon cow talk is more limited in quantity. It may be just a few cow sounds, making it difficult to pick them out from the bird sounds and tough to home in on them.

Another time when elk sounds are more frequent is when they are either on the move or getting ready to move. As a result, making cow sounds of your own is a good strategy when moving through the timber. It helps disguise your own travel as that of a cow on the move and increases the chances you'll get a reply to help you in locating the elk.

All of this, of course, relies on the fact that a hunter has a well-practiced ear which is capable of sorting out the different sounds in the mountains.

A good example of my own years of experience, vast knowledge of the mountains, the ability to pinpoint sounds, making a positive identification, and then closing in for that final stalk, came on a hunt some years back. Three of us heard a bull bugling about five-hundred yards away from us and answered his call. For the next

Out in the open, one bull herd reacted to a single cow call from nearly a mile away. Ron Shade photo.

fifteen minutes, we bugled back and forth, but the bull never moved. We decided to go after him, moving slowly through the timber toward the place where the bull kept answering us.

After closing in on our bull, we found out the bugling was actually being made by two hunters from Great Falls. The other guy who answered my calls was an excellent bugler. And, for his part, he figured he was onto a good bull as well. It had taken about an hour for the two hunting groups to get together and when we did, there were a few laughs and a good visit that followed.

So don't be surprised if even your trained ear is fooled. It's really the ultimate compliment to an elk caller to have other hunters consider him to be an elk. And there have been times when I've called and had camp robbers fly in and make perfect imitations of the cow talk I was making. That, too, makes a hunter wonder if his well-practiced ear might not need a little more practice.

The fact that birds make sounds very similar to elk might simply be nature's way of protecting the species from hunters like us. Without that protection, it would be relatively easy to identify and key in on such a distinctive sound.

As it is now, even an experienced hunter has to train his ears well to listen for cow talk. But the hunter who learns to listen can hear elk before he sees them and move in on them carefully so he doesn't have to hear that horrible bark.

Making Sense of Scents

Everyone has their own image of elk hunting. And, in their minds, the elk they go up against have special traits and defenses that these hunters must overcome. Personally, my favorite view of elk was quoted in the book, The Hunter's Guide to Montana. In a section of the book devoted to elk, Mike Fillinger, of Helena, summed up the animal he has chased for so many years this way: "All you have to do is remember they can hear everything within a mile, even a whisper. They can see everything at five miles, including the ants. And they can smell everything in the state of Montana."

Hunters go to great lengths to prepare themselves for their annual autumn assault on these elk defenses. They dress in quiet clothing and leave partners behind who talk too loudly in the woods or tend to wear items made of stiff nylon or corduroy. Bowhunters believe in wearing camouflage from their underwear to their overcoats and smear on greasy goo to hide their faces and hands.

But the biggest mystery of the sensual battle with elk is the use of odors to lure them in or confuse their noses. Look through any catalog with a wide range of gear for the hunter and you're bound to bump into a variety of urine scents, sex scents, attracting scents, masking scents, scent pads, scent containers and things to eliminate scent. Some are made for deer, bear, and elk while others imitate fox, skunk, apples, acorns, cedars, pines, and even dirt. That they could come in such variety has always fascinated me, just as I've always wondered how they get big old elk to pee in those little bitty bottles.

Scent does play a role in elk hunting in several ways, both from the elk's point of view and the hunter's. We've already discussed the fact that elk use scent in many ways. It appears to play a role in elk finding other elk. It's a marking device at rubs and wallows. And bulls seem to want to impregnate their coats with it while wallowing, making themselves smell stronger during the rut than at any other time of year.

Their sense of smell is also crucial to their defense system. Like

Often, the ability to keep yourself scent-free depends on how you get into the back-country. Mark Henckel photo.

coyotes and other animals that come into a call, elk like to circle downwind from the source of the sounds to get a whiff of what's making all the noise. That way, their nose becomes an ally of their eyes and ears to identify or verify what those other senses have told them.

As a result, the first part of using scents in hunting is to eliminate your own. Hunters can accomplish this in several ways. Some hunters take their clothing and hang it outdoors for several weeks before the season to eliminate household odors. They pack it in plastic garbage sacks for the drive to and from their hunting trips as well. Some go as far as rolling it in, or packing it in a plastic bag with, elk droppings to give it an odor of its own. And there was one hunter I heard of who scoured the countryside for the first guy who shot an elk, begged the elk's scent glands off of him, then carried them around in his pockets for the rest of the season. The trouble with any of these approaches is that once a hunter has climbed his first mountain while wearing that clothing, it's soaked with his perspiration, too. Given enough soakings with sweat and that clothing is going to smell like an old armpit which wrestled an elk and lost.

The better rule of thumb for hunters is that cleanliness is next to elkliness. It's far easier to wash that clothing clean with a plain detergent between hunting trips than to keep adding elk scent to it. And a hunter has a far better chance of fooling an elk if his clothes are scent-free than if they're loaded with the wrong kind of scent.

The same thing is true of the hunters themselves. For day trips, the best way is to shower or bathe with a plain soap before heading into the field. That way, a hunter starts clean and even if he perspires, there won't be much time for the odor-spreading bacteria to grow on him. The problem is that often a hunter is in an elk camp situation where taking a daily shower is an impossibility. Sponge baths will help here, if the elk camp involves a travel trailer, motor home, or heated wall tent. Or, if the hunter is truly hardy, there may be a cold-running stream nearby. We've even been that tough in the past, going as far as washing our hair with some water straight from the creek. But not anymore. Frankly, we can't afford to freeze out any more brain cells than we have already lost. And the memory of splashing that ice-cold creek water into warm armpits is revisited only in my fondest nightmares.

A less-bracing alternative to keeping yourself clean in a hunting camp situation is the liberal use of baking soda. Baking soda kills odors remarkably well and can be used both as a cleansing solution and dusting powder. Mixed with water in camp, it can be used to wash the body to remove odors if your camping situation will allow it. Or it can be sprinkled on areas where a person is apt to perspire, like under the arms, on your forehead, inside your hatband, down your back, and even inside your shorts. After five or six days, a person can still prevent excessive human odor through the liberal application of baking soda. Your campmates might even thank you for using it. And it might even keep elk in the area that would have been scared away by all the screaming and shouting had you tried to wash up at the creek instead.

Keeping yourself clean of odors, rather than permeating yourself with them, allows a hunter to better use his own nose for hunting, too. Elk have a strong smell that can be picked up by the human nose. Bulls smell stronger than cows during autumn, primarily because of their activities during the rut. And hunters can pick up that smell from some distance as they move through the timber.

When you pick up the tell-tale scent of elk, the first thing to do is check the direction of the wind to determine which way the odor is coming from. Then, get ready. The source of that smell is very likely within fifty yards of you. It might be coming from the elk themselves and a hunter should be prepared for that. Just work through the area slowly, use your call, and be alert to signs that elk might be nearby.

The source of the smell could just as easily be coming from an elk wallow, which is valuable to the hunter, too. It would give a hunter an excellent place to call to bulls of that area. Or, the scent could be a sign of an elk bedding area.

Elk beds will hold their scent for a day or two, primarily because the bulls and cows urinate in them either while they are lying there or when they first stand up. Bulls are notorious for urinating on themselves while in their beds, as yet another way of strengthening their odor in autumn. In fact, when hunters take a bull in the rut, they should look for a patch of darker-colored, wet, or oily fur on the underside of the chest of the animal which marks this trait. That patch of hide and fur should be cut off when field-dressing the bull to reduce the chances of it rubbing against meat and tainting its taste.

Cow Talk

Bulls give off a strong odor during the rut and a hunter should be able to smell them. Ron Shade photo.

While we've concentrated our discussion on eliminating human odors and keeping a clear nose to smell the elk around us, commercial elk scents do have a place in our scheme of things. They can be an invaluable ally when used in moderation at the right time. That time is when you expect to have a close encounter with elk at any moment.

When I jump a group of elk, cow call to them, and figure I've stopped them, then it's time to pull out the elk scent. The same thing is true if I've been calling and get a reply. I'll sprinkle commercial elk urine on my pant legs and on the camo covers on the limbs of my bow. It doesn't take much, when first applied, to saturate the area with elk smell and mask my own odor.

Some hunters have taken this plan of attack one step further and filled atomizers with elk urine. When they get into calling situations where they figure an elk will be coming in soon, they spray the air around them to spread the scent through the area. That certainly will mask human odor when the elk come in for a look.

Put it all together and it makes sense of scents. Keep yourself clean so they can't smell you. Don't over-use scents so you can smell them. Then pull out the scent to cover your own odor when you think you're due for a close encounter. Do it that way and it might mean the difference between pulling them in close enough for a shot or having them get away from you while they're still out of range.

But whatever you do, stay away from bathing in those cold mountain creeks. They're bad for the body, worse for your vocabulary, and the suds don't look too good floating downstream, either. Save that high country bathing for your nightmares, for the guys who do soak themselves in elk scent, or for that partner in the stiff nylon coat and the corduroy pants.

The Sneak

It was while doing some film work with wildlife cinematographer Gordon Eastman that another benefit of the cow call was discovered. Eastman, of Powell, Wyo., had his eye on some big bull elk which would fit in well with a video cassette he was producing on cow calling, entitled "How To Talk To The Elk." But we had a problem. Between us and the bulls, there was a big herd of cows.

If you use a cow call, the elk will often ignore the sounds you make while moving. Ron Shade photo.

The situation was not unlike many that a hunter faces during the archery and rifle seasons. With such a high percentage of any elk population being made up of cows, it's sometimes difficult to get past them to within striking distance of the bull. Often, their eyes, noses and ears are the ones that protect him. The hunter doesn't scare the bull. Instead, one of the cows with him sounds the alarm and spooks the whole herd, other cows, calves, and the bull included.

On the film trip with Eastman, we had to cross a large and open sagebrush hillside to reach the bulls. But the cows were scattered in the nearby timber with a clear view of anything that crossed the hillside.

The answer was cow calling quite frequently, making a call every thirty seconds, waiting a short while, then doing it again. After going through the calling sequence for ten to fifteen minutes, there were four cows watching us and they all started talking back. Up in the timber, other cows chimed in. Then they all stopped and never answered again, though I continued my calling.

Finally, a bull stepped out into view 200 yards away and started feeding. Still out in the open, Eastman and I could do little but keep going, trying to get closer as I continued calling. By the time we were done, we had walked to within fifty yards before the bull looked up. When he did, the bull could hardly believe his eyes. The cow he was sure had been there, suddenly turned into the horrifying vision of two men within spitting distance. The bull swapped ends instantly when he realized his mistake and roared out of there.

The cow talk had actually covered our movements. After the initial cow sounds, the elk had accepted the fact that there were other elk in the area and gave it little thought. They figured that all the sounds of our walking and the movements we made were just part of those new elk that had wandered in.

Since that day, the same cow call strategy has worked often on elk while making a sneak. A bull call never would. Those bull calls are issued as a challenge or a means of advertising for cows to come over and join a harem. Even in a rutting situation, the bull call wouldn't do it as well. While they might tolerate the calling, one sour note and the sneak would be over. The cow call, on the other hand, is no challenge at all. It's just idle conversation between elk, a sign of reassurance. And when you make a sour note on the cow call, just wait a second and call again. It doesn't seem to bother them.

As a result, cow talk is literally a way to cover your tracks. When you step on a stick or kick loose a rock while making a sneak, just blow on the cow call and they'll think an elk made the noise. The key is that three-call sequence, spaced thirty seconds apart.

It's the answering sound you need to accomplish the sneak. The cow talk is enough to make them drop their wariness and keep them from feeling threatened.

The strategy here is to go after them, without making them feel compelled to come to you. All you want to do is answer their calls, not locate them or bring them in. And for this, the cow call works in all seasons. It has worked for me in the summer. It has worked in the fall. And Rob Seelye, a Laurel bowhunter, has even done it during a late bowhunt when snow covered the ground and he was camouflaged in white.

That doesn't mean, of course, that a hunter can totally ignore making noise or blending in with his surroundings. In truth, cow calling in a sneak situation works best when the elk don't see you. Their eyes would have to be classified as their major defense mechanism and they can spot things amiss at a long distance. Hearing and smell are important, too, but these senses can be fooled more easily by the hunter. An elk rarely sticks around when there's danger he can see.

Camouflage clothing is always a good bet to get around that defense, if your hunting regulations allow it. That means wearing camouflage pants, coat, and hat, and includes covering your face and hands with face paint or netting. Your hands and face, in fact, act like a shining beacon for wildlife to spot you if they're not covered. They are your body parts most likely to move in a hunting situation and are probably the first things which are spotted by wildlife.

In terms of clothing, most fabrics also seem designed for failure. The emphasis these days is on wind-breaking or rain-shedding or extreme durability. These fabrics often rustle when you move or sing out a warning when a branch rubs across them. Look instead for the softer fabrics which won't rustle or make noise in the mountains. Wear these in most situations, then stuff a rainsuit in your hunting pack for the times when the weather really does turn bad on you.

Boots are much the same. The hard soles of most boots on the market make the steps of a single hunter walking sound more like a regiment on the march. They grind rocks. They break sticks. They thump on hard ground. And, in doing that, they act like an early warning system, telegraphing every step of the hunter to the elk's receptive ears. It's better to go soft when buying a pair

Camouflage clothing and face paint will help hide you from the sharp eyes of the elk. Mark Henckel photo.

of boots for elk hunting. Some hunters have even opted for running shoes or high-topped sneakers as their footwear of choice. But for many of us, those shoes don't offer enough support for hiking the uphills, downhills, and sidehills that the elk call home. Look instead for the type of boot that lends you enough support for your needs, but still offers some softness underfoot. There are no hard and fast rules to this, especially in a marketing age where new materials and designs seem to come out of the warehouse to the sporting goods dealers on a yearly basis. Just rest assured that if you go soft, you'll be happy you did the next time you get into a sneak situation.

And finally, keep a low profile. Elk react quickly to the upright figure of a man moving through the timber or out in the open spaces. It's a shape they have grown to recognize and fear over the years with good reason. By staying low when you move and kneeling when you call, the hunter is far less obvious to them. And go slowly. Unless the elk are moving out in front of you, it's likely that they'll stay put until you get to where you want to go. If you sneak too quickly and spook them in the process, your speed won't be rewarded anyway.

All you have to do to make the scene complete is to mix in enough cow calls to make them think that it's really an elk making those slow movements and creating those subtle noises. If you play your elk part well, you just might end up with the sneak of a lifetime, on the bull of your dreams.

Curiosity Kills the Elk

The situation had all the earmarks of premature disaster. I had been hunting in the snow in the Bob Marshall Wilderness, trying to drum up some enthusiasm in elk that were less than enthusiastic about a fresh coat of foot-deep snow. It was September then, a time in previous years when we had soaked up the beauties of warm fall afternoons and bugling bulls on frosty mornings.

This year, I was openly dejected about packing in twenty miles on horseback, only to have the world snow on my bowhunting parade for four straight days. Hunting hadn't been good and spending day after day in sloppy fall snow wasn't making the trip any better.

Walking with my head down and leaning into the force of the snow and wind, I wasn't really paying much attention to the world around me. Until the cow barked. When I looked up, there were a dozen elk including a good five-point bull not two-hundred yards away. They were watching me when a young cow in the middle of the herd gave an inquisitive call again. They had me cold,

This aptly-named brush bull wears something he picked up along the way. Ron Shade photo.

standing erect out in the middle of a meadow, with my bow at my side. With no real hope of trying any kind of sneak on them, I slipped a diaphragm call in my mouth and simply called back, trying to imitate the sound the cow had made. She perked up her ears at this, paused for a while, then called again. Once again I answered her.

This give and take between man and elk lasted for the next fifteen minutes. In the process, the rest of the herd started feeding while the young cow craned her neck and used a high-stepping walk to slowly close the distance between us. When she finally gave up, barked her displeasure, and spooked the herd, she was barely seventy-five yards away. That's still well out of my bow range, but close enough to provide a warm, vivid memory amid the snow and cold that chills the rest of my recollections of the hunting trip.

The incident came about before elk hunters knew much about cow talk. There were bugles from bulls and barks from cows and everything else was just a variation on that theme or a sour note the elk made. Without realizing it, I had my initiation into making cow talk and learning how it works on the curious nature of elk.

In retrospect, I can say the young cow played her part well in the little drama that unfolded twenty miles back in from the trailhead.. Being young, the cow was unsure of herself and wandered to within what would certainly have been fatal range for virtually anyone packing a firearm. It was curiosity over the cow call in its purest form.

Looking back at it, I can also figure out what fooled her eyes. It was the snow. Though I was standing erect, the front of my camouflage clothing was well-spattered with snow. That was just enough to break up my outline. And as long as I stood still, it was enough to make her doubt what she was seeing.

This curious nature of elk goes against much of what hunters think about them. Too often, they're given a list of traits that makes them seem like Superman in a shaggy tan coat. They've got the eyes of an antelope, the ears of a mule deer, the smelling ability of a black bear, and the temperament of a whitetail. Put it all together and call it an elk and you have an animal that's virtually impossible to fool. That description is just not true and anyone who has spent much time in the elk woods knows it. Certainly, elk have very capable defenses, but their curious and sometimes trusting nature can be used against them by the hunter who wants to fill his freezer with prime eating.

A hunting acquaintance whose name I can't remember, told me some years ago about an experience he had after dousing some elk urine scent on his pantlegs. He walked all day through the elk woods hearing occasional grunting and groaning sounds behind him. And all day, he turned around but was unable to spot the source of the noise. Finally, while crossing a big basin, he turned around to spot a spike bull making the noise some distance behind him. Unfortunately, the spike bull saw him, too, and he never got a shot. But the spike's curiosity would have been his undoing had the hunter realized what was making the noise.

In defense of that hunter, it should be pointed out that these curious elk often get the better of us. We have ingrained in ourselves so deeply the notion that elk are tough, that we are rarely prepared for the ones that come willingly. There was one time when I was hunting with Vince Yannone, of Helena, that a cow came in so fast it caught both of us unprepared. We had just hiked into an area, capping off the move with a climb of a steep slope covered with broken timber. We sat for a moment, catching our breath, and Yannone cupped his hands around his mouth and gave a call. Before either of us could react, a cow came racing up the slope at a dead run, stopped for a second behind a small pine thirty yards in front of us, then turned tail and ran back down the hill just as fast as it came. Neither of us had our bows ready. Neither of us could do anything but look at each other in amazement at an opportunity for which we had both climbed a steep slope only to be unprepared when an inquisitive elk answered his call.

Why one cow will often take it upon herself to do the investigating is a mystery. But often they do roar in just that quickly to discover the source of the sound. At times they'll come in with company, too, bringing in another cow or even the whole herd with them.

The cow call can turn out to be the invaluable tool of the hunter in trying to arouse this curiosity. In some respects, that's because we don't really know what we're telling them with a cow call. It's their language, but the exact meanings of specific sounds are still unknown to us. Perhaps when we hit certain notes, it triggers a response in them that an elk is injured or in need of quick help. Perhaps it's just that some elk are more responsive to cow sounds than others. We know that all elk are individuals and they react to specific sounds in different ways. Like humans, some are simply more gullible or excitable than others.

In terms of trying to explain the times that many elk respond, it's only logical that when the whole herd comes in, we have piqued the curiosity of the lead cow. If a hunter can get her to come to the call, he can bring everything else in with her, bulls included. The importance of that lead cow can't be underestimated in any book on elk. She is his best friend and his worst enemy. She is the smartest and wariest and toughest of the elk. If a hunter can get the better of that lead cow, he has a good chance to virtually pick and choose from anything else he wants in the rest of the herd.

Elk curiosity exhibits itself in other ways, too. Bulls especially get themselves into some of the darndest situations simply because they let their inquisitive nature get the better of them.

Outfitter Bill Hoppe, of Gardiner, was guiding a client in a late hunt once, who shot a good six-point bull that had entangled its antlers in about 40 feet of copper telephone wire. That telephone wire served its purpose in the old days when it was stretched to a ranger station far back in the mountains. How the elk became entangled in the wire is anyone's guess. But about twenty feet

It's not uncommon to run into elk carrying some type of wire in their antlers. Ron Shade photo.

of it was wrapped tightly around the antlers. The remaining twenty feet trailed behind the animal, rattling and banging off trees, rocks, and stumps.

As a result, the bull wasn't nearly as wary as he might have been. He had become so accustomed to the noise of that wire dragging behind him that he wasn't jumpy at all when the client moved in on him for a shot at relatively close range. At least, the six-point would normally have been far more suspicious of strange noises had he not been carrying his own noisemaker through the mountains.

Other bulls have been spotted with rope, woven wire, and barbed wire in their antlers. While some of them are easy to explain as accidents, it's hard to imagine that curiosity didn't come into play in some of their escapades. And their curious nature is something that a hunter can capitalize on, especially when using the cow call. And it's a personality trait hunters should be aware of whenever they're in elk country.

Calling Elk In The Early Rut

Hot bulls can be called in by almost anyone with almost any kind of call on the market. When they hit the peak of the breeding season, these bulls have been called in with everything from blowing into a spent rifle shell to the most expensive of calls on the market.

But what we're talking about here is lukewarm bulls. These are bulls in the time period before the peak of the rut. Their minds have started to begin thinking of cows and the breeding season that follows. Their bodies have started to react to the changes of the breeding season. The wallows are being used. Trees are being rubbed. And the mountain mornings have begun to have their frosty chill pierced by the bugles of bulls finding their voices.

It's an excellent time to be out in the elk woods. In fact, there are some hunters who wouldn't trade those days of early September for any other time, including the peak of the rut. These hunters feel their best chances of calling in a bull are found in this pre-rut period when harems are being formed and bulls are starting to feel their oats.

But hunters should be aware that bulls do act differently at this time than during the peak of the rut. In that peak period, it's possible to have a bull charge in to point-blank range, snorting and urinating and raking his antlers on the ground. The cows are coming into heat on a daily basis during that peak period and bulls are anxious to defend the herds they have in tow. In the pre-rut period, on the other hand, bulls tend to be a little more tentative in their approach to the hunter. They're not going to charge in. In fact, they may take a little coaxing and teasing to get them within range.

Last fall's hunt, on the opening day of the Montana archery season, provides the perfect example. Hunting wih a group of friends, I had bugled once from a divide before dropping into a basin and got no response. Halfway down the basin slope, I bugled again and got a faint answer in reply from about a half-mile away. My next bugle also went unanswered but a series of cow calls got a second bugle in return. Answering the elk with a bugle, a second bull chimed in. A few more cow calls produced another bugle which seemed to be closer. They were coming in.

What followed was a massive application of the cow call. After moving toward them, all of us began cow calling, bringing responses from cows and another bull. Two bulls finally emerged a hundred-fifty yards away coming in our direction. When they were at seventy-five yards, I squealed on a bull call and that made the final difference.

The bigger of the bulls finally stepped into an opening forty yards away, stopped as I made a cow call, and provided the shot I wanted. Hit through the lungs, he went just thirty-five yards before piling up in the timber below. He was a good bull, a six-by-four with one freak horn, that had a spread of forty-eight inches. But it gave me an awfully tough act to follow next season. Two years ago, I had taken my bull within five hours on opening day. This bull last year took just thirty-five minutes of the season. Next year, I'd be better off to hang up the bow and just tell everyone I don't want to show off by getting one any quicker.

The calling sequence involved with getting that bull shows how heavily a hunter must rely on the cow call during the pre-rut period. At times, the cow call will be enough to pull in a bull. At other times, it takes a mixture of cow talk and bull talk to get the job done.

It usually only takes a look at the calendar to tell a hunter if he's working in a pre-rut situation. The peak of the rut in most parts of the northern Rockies hits from the middle of September

Last fall's archery season was over in just thirty-five minutes of hunting. Don Laubach photo.

Typically, bull elk are still finding their bugling voices in the pre-rut period. Ron Shade photo.

through the first of October. Anyone hunting the first part of September is very likely in a pre-rut period.

But the peak of the rut is variable. It seems like the rut could be going full-bore in one drainage and be either before or after the peak in other areas, even in the same mountain range. One of the keys I always use to determine the rut is to watch the aspens in autumn. When the aspens are wearing their yellow leaves, the rut is usually in high gear. If the leaves are still green, figure that you're still in a pre-rut calling situation unless the elk tell you differently. Not that the elk are watching the aspen leaves. It's a matter of photoperiod, the length of the day, which triggers both the turning leaves and the elk entering their breeding season.

Another way to tell if you're in the pre-rut phase is to listen closely to the bulls that answer you. Typically, the elk are still finding their voices at this time of year. They're bugling. In fact, they may be bugling every bit as much as at the peak of the rut. But instead of the hoarse, raspy bugles complete with a series of grunts on the end, the pre-rut bull may only squeal at you. And even that squeal won't be at full volume.

Just because you get a half-hearted answer from a bull to your call doesn't necessarily mean the hunter is in a single-elk situation, either. Because the bulls are lukewarm at this time of year, it may take some coaxing on your part to get them to answer. In the case of the bull I shot last fall, our best guess estimate, based on what we heard and were able to reconstruct later, was that there was really a total of five bulls in that basin along with a good-sized herd of cows. Yet the fist time I bugled, I never got a single response. The second time I bugled, there was only one faint response. It was only after talking with the elk for a while that the other elk made their presence known.

The answer for the hunter who hopes to call in elk at this time of year is to be persistent, imitate the high-pitched squeal, forget about making grunts, and use the cow call liberally. That cow talk can accomplish several things for the hunter, giving the impression that there are plenty of cows there, too, that all is well in the elk woods, and that one of the cows in the area might have come into heat early and is receptive to the company of a bull.

Another thing is to never underestimate pre-rut calling. While the bulls may not be calling as much, they may actually be easier to lure within range. At the peak of the rut, the harem groups are already formed and the bulk of the big bulls' energies are being put into trying to keep their cows in line. In the pre-rut period, herd bulls are still adding to those cow groups. They're on the prod looking for more cows. There are also smaller brush bulls still wandering the country which are looking for their place in the scheme of things. And spikes, which are now in the process of being run out of the cow groups, are looking for any elk which will tolerate their company.

Because the bulls are so receptive in the pre-rut, a hunter may need only the cow call to get the job done. Hunters who have restricted their calling to cow talk have reported that the bulls actually came in less wary than on other occasions when only bull talk was used. Because there apparently was no challenger for the cow's affections, the bulls came in willingly with their guard down. As a result, they were more vulnerable for the hunter. And even when these bulls were spooked, hunters who blew the cow call at them again, often found the bulls would turn and come back for another look. Being less wary in the first place, they were easy to fool a second time into returning to verify what spooked them. It would usually take a strong whiff of man scent that second time around to discourage them and send them running. And some bulls have even been called in with cow talk a third time despite getting that whiff.

The main thing hunters should remember is not to be afraid of the pre-rut period. So often, they time their hunts to coincide with the peak of the rut and miss some of the better hunting of the season because of it. The pre-rut period is among the best of times to be in the elk woods for the hunter who has cow talk on his side.

■

BULL TALK

The sweet music of a bull elk's bugle is unlike any other sound in the wild. It is power. It is mystery. It is rugged grace. And it stirs men's souls to grab their rifle or bow and head to the high country.

Is it any wonder that an elk hunter's favorite time is the weeks of late September and early October when the bulls are at the peak of the rut. It's during that breeding season when the herd bulls are screaming their challenges, the brush bulls are feeling their first strong stirrings of the mating urge, and the spikes are getting their first taste of life on their own.

The peak of the rut can be the best of times to bring in a bull. That's when their bugling activity is at its fever pitch. It's when hunters have brought in bulls by doing nothing more than whistling with an empty rifle shell.

This is the time that mother nature made for elk hunters to join the bulls in their song. It's time to grab elk whistles, elk diaphragms and outside-the-mouth reed calls to make bull talk.

But to be a successful elk caller, it takes an understanding of the animals you're after, the places they go, and when they go there, in addition to knowing how to call.

Herd bulls, brush bulls, and spikes require different strategies from the hunter and are apt to react to the calls the hunter makes in their own unique ways. A hunter has to adapt his techniques to those differences, to know when to press a bull and when to be patient. He has to know where to position himself and how much calling is required to bring in a bull.

In short, the hunter has to know about the elk themselves at the peak of the rut, in addition to how to call them, if he's going to consistently find success with his bull talk.

Advertising By Bugle

It was almost like a dream. In its purest form, the bugle of a bull elk burst forth and cut the evening quiet. High, shrill, and pure, the bugle was the sweetest sound in the outdoors and was followed by a series of warlike grunts before being swallowed in the stillness.

Once again, the bugle burst forth. Then again. And again. And again. Then, whap, my wife hit me with a shoe from across the room, all but making me swallow my elk bugle in mid-toot.

"You blow on that thing one more time and the doctors will have to do a buglectomy on you," snarled the sweet thing I married so many years ago. "You blow on that thing again and you better hope you put a cow in the freezer this year because it's the only female companionship you're going to have this winter."

It did not appear to be an idle threat. I could tell because the second shoe was already in her uplifted hand and she was making grasping motions in the direction of the lamp. How she could be so unreasonable, I just don't know. Even the bad notes I was making on the elk bugle sounded pretty good to me. And I was finally getting to the point that the good notes were starting to outnumber the bad ones.

In any event, that's how I got started blowing my elk calls in the car on the way to and from work. It's a tolerable place to practice, even though I'm always guaranteed to get a few odd looks on every drive. People just don't seem to understand why I'm sucking on this vacuum cleaner hose or why I'm heaving my midriff up and down and making grunting noises. But I can live with it.

Learning to make bull talk is just part of the game hunters play

Hunters have experimented with a wide range of items to imitate the sound of a bull elk. Mark Henckel photo.

who want to call in elk in the autumn. It's a game they've been playing for years and one, I'm afraid, which has drawn the same less-than-rave reviews from wives throughout that span. But the bugling game has changed quite a bit during that time and so have the calls.

The first elk calls were really whistles aimed at reproducing the high-pitched notes achieved at the top of the elk bugle. These calls were either hand-made or bought commercially. The hand-made models were made with such things as copper tubing, bamboo, or plastic piping. A notch was cut in them, the end of the tube was either covered or plugged, and the caller simply blew into them. By increasing the amount of air pressure, they produced a rising crescendo of three or four notes.

One of the more interesting whistles was made with a mountain squash stalk and a willow plug. All the materials were there in the back country and it took just a pocket knife and a little experimentation to come up with a workable call.

Some hunters even called in bulls with spent rifle cartridges. By blowing across the top of them like a person would on a jug, they could produce a high-pitched whistle that would bring a response from the bulls.

Among the popular early commercial models was a straight tube whistle made by Herter's. Over the years, the design was copied by many manufacturers. Even today, the straight-tube elk whistle is among the more common seen in the mountains.

After the straight tube came, a length of brass or copper corrugated natural gas pipe. This was curled into about three or four wraps and the caller simply blew into one end of it. The end result was a high-pitched whistle made by air rushing over the corrugated surface.

The problem was that there wasn't much volume to the call. And, like the straight-tube whistle, it was easily recognizable in the mountains. It didn't really sound much like an elk, just a whistle. But, like the whistle, it didn't take much practice and was easy to use. Just pucker up and blow and the call did the rest of the work.

But don't write these calls off, even today. Over the years, they accounted for plenty of the elk being taken in the bow and gun seasons. They invariably relied on hitting the peak of the rut to do much good. The bull had to be hot, to come in close. More often, when the bulls weren't real hot, they'd answer and might even come in some distance, but they wouldn't respond well enough to come in real close.

The first of the new wave calls was nothing more than a straight tube made of plastic, fiberglass, or corrugated tubing. From an inch to an inch-and-a-half in diameter, these so-called grunt tubes didn't make any notes on their own. They were simply used for resonance and the grunts and squeals were made from the hunter's own throats.

It took plenty of practice and sometimes some pain to become an accomplished practitioner of the grunt tube. The reason for this is that all the calls were made on the inhale, forcing air through the voice box the wrong way. Vince Yannone, of Helena, was one of the best I knew of, in terms of fooling elk. He didn't even use a tube for resonance, just cupped his hands around his mouth and made elk talk. But it was brutal on his throat. Part of his standard hunting gear was several rolls of Life Savers. And he told me once he inhaled so hard in making a call that he heard something pop and the entire front of his throat later went black-and-blue from the damage.

But hunters who could use the grunt tube well were deadly on elk. Their squeals, bugles, and grunts were unlike any commercial call on the market and were closer to the sounds the elk were making than those made by anyone packing a whistle. But they took plenty of hours of practice and some throat-stretching in the weeks before the season for the hunter who used them effectively.

The big breakthrough in calling came when someone discovered that diaphragm turkey calls could make elk noises. That these turkey calls worked, was a well-guarded secret of the few for a number of years. They were, in fact, the first commercially-made calls that allowed a hunter to actually bugle for elk. By pressing them to the roof of your mouth and regulating the tension on the latex diaphragm with your tongue, these calls made a wide range of elk noises. They reproduced the high-pitched bugle. They imitated the grunts and squeals. And they even made the cow-calf sounds though few of the early diaphragm callers realized how effective those sounds could be.

The first of the diaphragm calls actually sold for elk, were really little more than re-packaged turkey calls. But these calls often blew out quickly. The stress and strain of producing the elk noises put uncommon stress on the latex diaphragms. On one week-long hunting trip, I popped a new call in my mouth on the first day and by day seven, it was virtually worthless for making elk sounds. At four or five dollars a pop, it was possible to go through twenty dollars or more worth of calls in a season of practicing and field use.

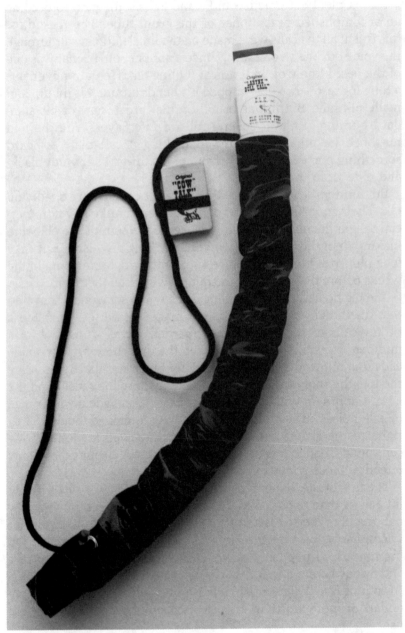

Outside-the-mouth elk calls using latex bands are the new kids on the block. Don Laubach photo.

On another occasion, I can remember a hunting trip that was cut short because the vibrating diaphragm actually split my tongue. I was out of business until the tongue healed.

The diaphragm calls were best when used in conjunction with a grunt tube. And, like the tube, they took plenty of practice. Hours and hours and hours on mid-summer drives were spent blowing on the diaphragm calls to get good at them. Some callers never did get the hang of it either, because the diaphragm calls didn't fit correctly in the mouth, brought on gag reflexes by the hunters, or were simply too tough to master. But for those who learned, did they ever work. Hunters brought bulls within spitting distance before, during, and after the rut with diaphragm calls. But they paid dearly for it in practice time.

If there's a new wave of elk bugles on the scene, it's the exterior diaphragm calls. These combine the ease of being able to blow, rather than inhale, and get the diaphragm outside the mouth. These, too, are usually used in conjunction with a grunt tube and make some amazingly beautiful elk music. They take more practice than the old elk whistles but far less than the inside-the-mouth diaphragms. The best of these calls allow the hunter to make an excellent imitation the actual bugling of the bulls. They rely on latex rubber bands or some other types of reed to make their bull sounds.

Calls like E.L.K., Inc.'s "Larynx Bull Call" are the new kid on the block and if early results are any indication, they should work just as well as the old turkey calls and the new inside-the-mouth elk diaphragms which are built a bit stronger to hold up longer. They make a sound just like the squeal, bugle, and grunts of a bugling bull and will fool even the big herd bulls when put in skilled hands.

The important thing, though, isn't so much the bugle a hunter is using. It's a matter of whether or not he can find the elk to use it on. It's whether or not the elk are receptive to being called. And, finally, it's how much practice the hunter is willing to put in with the call of his choice.

For that practice, I always head back to the trusty automobile and the drives to and from work. That may make for some odd stares from people in other cars or pedestrians on the street. But it sure beats cuddling up to a frozen cow elk when the winter winds blow.

The King And His Court

Think of a big herd bull as a stud with woman problems. There he is, surrounded by all the loveliest ladies of the mountains, flashing their come-along smiles, showing a little elk thigh, and promising some wild times in the woods when the time is right.

The stud is definitely excited about the prospects. But he's greedy, too. He wants as many of these wild women as he can get. He'll add to his harem with as many cows as he can grab and bugle out his invitations for more.

But all things are not going well for the big bull. He has grabbed almost more than he can handle. The cows he has so carefully gathered tend to wander a bit. It's almost like they're playing hard to get. In their coy cow manner, they move away from the herd and need to be forced back into the group.

Just to complicate matters, there are other suitors about. Satellite bulls are attracted to the big herds, bugling their own invitations and moving in on the flanks whenever the old boy is away. These bulls need to be whipped into shape, too, and the stud has to put the run on them and answer their bugles with harsh words of his own. If he can't bluff them with his bugles, he hooks them with his antlers. If they still don't keep their distance, they're playing with their lives.

So it goes with the elk world during the rut. The big bulls are constantly harrassed by other bulls and worried by the wandering of his cows. For several weeks in September and October, the king is constantly on the run trying to keep his court in order.

The bulls we're talking about here are the biggest of the big. These are the animals at the peak of their prime. In terms of age, the biggest bulls are between seven-and-a-half and ten-and-a-half years of age. These are the bulls of which Boone and Crockett Club records are made. In most places, they are a rare prize indeed. And one of the reasons they are rare is because of the demands of the rut.

Even the herd bulls that come into the rut in the best of shape, will drain their bodies of fat reserves and deplete their overall condition. By the time the rut ends, they will enter the late fall and winter in such poor shape, that they make themselves vulnerable to winter kill and predation. They run, they chase, they hook, they worry, and they fight during the weeks of the rut.

It's a busy enough scene that one wonders how any breeding ever gets done by the herd masters. There just doesn't seem to be any time for it with all the other things that are going on.

I watched just such a scene in a high mountain meadow some years back. It was out in the open stretched over an area of about three city blocks with a big herd bull managing a herd of about forty cows. Three cows on one end kept trying to move down the drainage. Three others on the other end of the herd didn't want to leave a feeding area. Complicating the issue, was a rival bull further up the drainage that kept bugling his presence.

When the cows started going down the creek drainage, the big six-point had to run down there, hook a few cows, and move them back up. When the other bull bugled up above, he had to run back up there, hook those cows in the flank and move them back. As he ran through the herd, the other cows moved out of his way to avoid similar hookings. By the time he had the upper cows in line, the lower cows were moving again. And by the the time he had the lower cows in line, the upper cows were moving again.

For an hour, he kept going back and forth through his herd trying to get them heading in the direction he wanted. Finally, they appeared to go there, heading off over a hill. But it was the disposition of the bull that was most amazing during the hour I watched him. His frustration level seemed to grow, the more he ran, and chased, and hooked his cows. And the other bull further up the drainage, which kept bugling and moving closer, just added to his problems and increased his anxiety.

Art Hobart, a Billings bowhunter, recalled an elk trip he made to Montana's Missouri Breaks where he bumped into a similar herd bull. He was hunting on an island in the river bottoms where a huge bull was trying to keep his cows in line. Because the bottoms were covered with a tangled mass of head-high willows, all he could see was the tall seven-by-eight rack of the bull when he closed to within about fifty yards of him. But he heard the bull bugling and thrashing the brush as he worked his cows. He watched the willows part at his passing. And, when a smaller six-point tried to invade the herd, Hobart heard the devastating crash and saw the bull come flying out of the willows sideways when the herd master struck him with his antlers to drive him away.

Herd bulls burn off their fat reserves chasing cows and keeping their harems in line. Michael Sample photo.

The only real defense a herd bull has against these invasions is to keep his cows close together, and keep them moving until he finds a place where they aren't bothered by other bulls. And that's a difficult task. The odor of cows coming into heat does more than just excite the herd bull. As the scent of a big herd of cows wafts through the mountains, it lures other bulls, too. Throw in the pressures exerted on the herds by hunters, and the urge to move becomes even stronger.

The question, then, becomes one of where to go? The herd bulls will try to find places where their frustrations are fewest. They'll move until they find areas where it's easier for them to keep the cows in line. They'll move until they find areas with few other bulls. And they'll move until they find areas without hunters.

But moving a big herd of cows isn't easy. The cows have minds of their own when it comes to where they want to go. And while they'll do their best to avoid the hooking antlers of the big bulls, they exert their influence on the direction of movements, too.

While it may seem to stack up as an adversary relationship between the herd bull and his cows, it should be pointed out that it really isn't entirely this way. Genetics, over time, have favored the system that dictates that the biggest and strongest of the bulls will produce the biggest and strongest calves. Cows will favor the best bulls at breeding time, as a result.

The cows also seem to show some allegiance to these bulls. Compared to the fevered chases of the night and morning, when the bull tries to keep his cows together, the bedding hours during the day are tranquil times. The herd bulls will be surrounded by cows when they're bedded and satellite bulls may even show up on the edges of these bedding groups. All the elk are napping together.

When the elk are bedded like this, the cows act as an early-warning system for their herd master. Any threat must pass through the cows first, before it reaches the big bull. As a result, the avid bull hunter has a tough task ahead of him, especially if the herd master is big enough to command a sizable number of cows.

While it's easy to understand that these cows wouldn't tolerate the sight or smell of a hunter, it's a fact that they don't like the invasion of a rival bull too well either. That may simply be because they don't like surprises on their bedding ground. It could also be that they feel an allegiance toward the herd bull. Or, it could be that they know the big bull will come out hooking with his antlers and they're the ones likely to be hooked. But one thing is sure. They certainly don't like it.

I recall one such incident when I spotted a good sized herd of elk bedded in the timber about a hundred yards away. The herd bull was right in the middle, relying on his cows to tell him of danger. I quietly crawled to within close range, before pulling out my elk call and bugling a challenge. Before that sound even had a chance to echo, the cows closest to me exploded out of there, taking the rest of the herd with them. They never saw me. They never smelled me. But the sound of that new bull in the area was enough to spook the whole herd.

Those old herd bulls can be had, of course, but it takes a different strategy than a sudden sneak attack. It was that rival bull up the drainage, working in on the herd bull and forty cows I talked about earlier, that had one angle on working the king and his court. That bull bugled the entire hour that I watched the herd, gradually working closer and closer. As time went on, it agitated the herd bull to the point that he was spoiling for a fight. And I'm sure that had the other bull made his entrance, the herd bull would have made a move to put the run on him.

Bulls will readily use their antlers to hook cows to get them to do what they want. Ron Shade photo.

An even safer line of attack would be to use the cow call. By making cow and calf sounds, the herd bull would figure that a member of his harem had wandered away. Or, perhaps, he might think that there's a new cow in the neighborhood and, wishing to add to his harem, he would come in to hook her into the group.

In addition to making a softer approach, the timing of that move on the herd bull would be far better than sneaking in on him in a bedding ground situation. The key is to work on the herd bull when he's up and agitated. Move in on him gradually and let his frustration work to your benefit. Then use your cow talk and bull talk wisely to lure him in for a shot.

Often, when these shots come, they will test a hunter's nerves more than anything else. A monster bull closing to within a few yards is a sight to behold. When he hooks the brush with his antlers, rakes the ground with them, and screams his challenges right into your ear, it's time for nerves of steel and steady fingers on the trigger or bowstring.

What you have is nearly a half-ton of rut-crazed bull before you, spoiling for war with an invader or looking to hook a cow back into the pack. That's one angry warrior or the unhappiest of hookers, depending on which way you look at it. And it's the type of situation which can force a bad shot by even the best of hunters. But, even if you miss, it's the kind of experience that will give you a memory you're not likely to forget for the rest of your hunting life.

Brush Bulls

Young whipper-snappers, that's what they are. No respect for their elders. No compassion for the kids. And no time to properly court a female before trying to get what they can from her. These are the brush bulls which wander the mountains of autumn, causing misery in the elk world wherever they go.

Brush bulls are the raghorns, the small two, three, four, five, and six-points, which are still too young to enter the breeding scene of the rut, but want to be part of it in the worst of ways. They're usually two to five years old, just old enough to feel the first juices of the rut flowing inside them and show an interest in the cows coming into heat.

But there's really no place for them in the peak of the rut. The herd bulls started their breeding season early, rounding up their harems of cows and keeping them on the move in search of hiding places where no other suitors would find them. The cows really don't want them either. In mother nature's scheme of things, genetic success dictates that the cows' best fortunes in producing the best calves lie with the herd bulls. For their part, the brush bulls don't tolerate the spikes. They know enough, that other bulls in the neighborhood means unwanted competition, even if the only competition around happens to be a spike.

As a result, the brush bull's role becomes one of a lone wanderer. He roams the open meadows, the deadfalls, black timber, and everywhere in between. He's spoiling for a fight, but knows he's going to lose. He wants his own herd of cows, but knows he can't hold them if they're ready to be bred. So, all through autumn, he bugles out his advertisements, challenges, and miseries to whoever will listen to them.

These brush bulls can be found anywhere during the rut. Their stopping place, eventually, will be hooking up with a herd bull and his band of cows. But it may take them a while to get there.

While the herd bulls grab their cows and go early in the rut, the brush bulls are still sparring with their mates and testing their voices. When the rutting urge hits them, they'll already be behind in the game. They'll be forced to wander the mountains in search of cows. In the process, they'll leave a trail of random rubs along their travel routes. These rubs are likely going to be closer to the ground than the ones made by the big herd bulls. They're often quick rubs, too, with relatively few strokes of the antler compared to the ones made by the big bulls which will completely girdle a tree. At times, a hunter will hit an area with a variety of these rubs. Some will be made this year, some last year, and some from years before that, designating a rub area that's frequented by brush bulls every year.

Brush bulls can get lucky, of course. Sometimes, they'll have a small harem of cows with them before the rut. But the brush bull doesn't have much luck in holding them unless he's got them in the most peculiar of places. Rather than the persuasive antlers and expertise of the big bulls, a brush bull can't hook a cow as effectively and keep her in line. So the herds are more likely to move at the whim of the cows. And with the brush bull showing off his bugling skills, it's only a matter of time before those cows wander within the realm of a herd bull. When that takes place, it's the brush bull which is run off, while his harem becomes absorbed into that of the herd bull.

When the brush bull loses his cows, he has only two choices before him. He can hang around and become a satellite bull of the herd. He'll bugle his challenges and become a pest that the herd bull really doesn't need. So the herd bull will try to run him

Brush bulls want cows of their own but don't have the age and size to hold them. Michael Sample photo.

off. And run him off. And run him off. Faced with that, the brush bull can either stick around and try his luck or take off again in search of more cows of his own.

Because the brush bulls are so fiesty and inexperienced at the game they are playing, they become easy prey for the hunter making bull talk. They'll answer almost anything. They'll come in strong. And, because they're so often alone, they're more vulnerable than the herd bull which has the eyes, ears, and noses of his harem to protect him.

What makes this variety the easiest of the bulls to call in is their solitary nature. If the brush bull gets lucky, on the other hand, it can be a far different story. A brush bull with three or four cows in tow knows he's getting the best of mother nature. He's got everything to lose, and nothing to gain, in taking on another bull. With a bugle alone, a hunter is never going to get a brush bull with cows within range.

Take that same bull and put him by himself or as a satellite of a big herd and it's a different story. Especially if you can stumble into a herd situation with plenty of satellite bulls.

Bozeman's Keith Wheat and I happened upon just such a situation in the Gallatin River drainage during an early rifle season more than two decades ago. It was back in the elk whistle days, but the realism of the sounds we made wasn't all that critical on this day.

We started bugling from a ridge at mid-afternoon and got an immediate answer. It took an hour to get down in the basin, and by the time we did, the elk had quit bugling. We got in an open park, propped our rifles against a tree, and decided to lay down for a rest. After a time, Wheat bugled as hard as he could and before the sound died, a bull stood at the other end of the park. It was a brush bull not seventy-five yards away, that ran right at us. We scrambled for the guns, but the bull had taken off before we could get off more than one quick shot.

Even before we looked to see if we hit the elk, Wheat whistled again and got three other bulls to answer. I followed up the shot, heading in the direction of one of the bugling bulls. Wheat went high, toward the area from which the other two bugles had come.

I followed the elk we shot at, finding no signs of blood. So I went after the bull we heard in that direction, walking a small trail until I spotted him looking at me from forty yards away. He ran, too, before I could get off a shot.

Wheat's three shots from up above made my decision of where to go next. Figuring he must have connected on one of the bulls with that much shooting, I walked in his direction only to be met by still another bull that ran past me through the trees. I finally hooked up with Wheat and found he had shot one of the bigger bulls we had ever seen.

It was the herd bull which he spotted with his binoculars and nailed in its bed as he was working up through the timber. Unfortunately, that was in the days before we really worried very much about Boone and Crockett Club records. Yet the numbers that bull's heavy, heavy rack produced still stick in my mind to this day. The royal point was twenty-seven inches long. The eyeguards were twenty inches. It had a fifty-five-inch main beam and a fifth-five-inch inside spread. The bases were fourteen inches in circumference, the same as Wheat's biceps at the time. The rack was a big one, indeed.

But, as I said, this was in the days before we really cared about record book scoring. And we did have quite a climb out of that basin to get the meat back to civilization. So we left the antlers behind, sticking them up in a tree.

Wheat went back into the basin the next year and retrieved the antlers, though a porcupine did a little damage to them in the meantime. He kept those antlers in his garage for a number of years before trading them for a 243 caliber rifle. But I'll never forget it. It was the biggest bull I have ever seen on the ground.

In retrospect, I can see in my mind what was happening in that basin. Wheat had stumbled onto the herd bull in its bed, surrounded by about forty cows. The bulls that I kept seeing below him, were the brush bulls, the satellites to that herd.

Had I known then what I know now, I'm sure we both could have filled our tags easily with our rifles. The brush bulls were so willing that they could be worked easily with bull talk and cow talk. It was simply a fluke that Wheat happened to stumble onto the herd bull in its bed. But those brush bulls had been plentiful, available, and easy.

Using a mixture of bull talk and cow talk is really the way to go when working on a brush bull. They'll answer the bull talk and come in to that alone more readily than any other class of bulls in the mountains. Find a loner and the hunter has a good chance of bringing him in. It's when the brush bulls have a few

Keith Wheat was able to find the giant herd bull while my time was spent with satellites. Don Laubach photo.

cows that things are more difficult for the caller. For that, a combination strategy of bull and cow talk might work, while cow talk alone is the surest best to arouse their innocent passions.

The thing to remember about brush bulls is that they are the frustrated lovers of the elk world. They want cows in the worst way. They are always bragging their prowess with their bugles. They're shadowing the big herds. Or they're looking for harems of their own. As such, they're suckers for a good caller and might even come in to someone not quite so sharp with a call. They're the bull you're most likely to pull in with your calls, when you hunt the peak of the rut.

Spikes

Pity the poor spikes. They are the babes of the woods. And that autumn of their spike year is the most vulnerable time of their entire bull lives.

Spikes have just reached puberty when the hunting season

arrives. They're out on their own, often for the first time. And other than knowing how to feed, sleep, and wander, their mission in life is really very unclear to them.

Spikes are yearling bulls which are going through their first real experience with a hunting season. A year ago, when they were calves, they were at their mother's side. Their mothers watched out for their needs. They signaled the danger. And, as if their mothers weren't enough, there was the security of the herd to protect them, even in the breeding season.

That situation changes when the bulls reach spike status. When the cow groups break up near summer's end and the herd bulls begin gathering their harems, the spikes are soon driven away. The herd bulls don't want them around. The spikes are left to wander. They're footloose and on their own, looking for companionship. When the spikes seek that companionship from a brush bull, they are driven away again. In fact, just about the only other elk that won't drive spikes away are other spikes.

When the breeding season arrives, a hunter is likely to run into singles or groups of yearlings. Most of these yearlings will be spikes, but some will also sport spindly, raghorn racks of two, three, or four points. Genetics and the amount of forage available in particular years will dictate how quickly a yearling's antler growth develops. But beneath that headgear lies the brain of a spike, no matter how many points he can brag about.

More and more these days, a hunter may run into a spike keeping the company of a cow or several cows. This is rare in elk country with a good cross-section of bulls of all ages. It's also rare in terms of traditional views of a spike's place in the scheme of things. In elk country where few mature bulls survived the previous hunting season, however, the situation can be different. While spikes have always been looked upon as the children of the elk world, biologists have found that they can and do breed cows in the absence of other bulls. If spikes are all that are left in the country, cows will accept being bred by them.

In a normal, mixed bull population, however, that isn't likely to happen. Spikes there tend to be non-aggressive, if there are any bigger bulls around. That may be simply because they are pushed around so much by the brush and herd bulls in the process of kicking them out of the herds. It wouldn't take too many pokes in the ribs from a big set of antlers to discourage a spike. Or, their

Spike bulls get no respect, like this one with a magpie perched on its head. Michael Sample photo.

non-aggressive nature could be the simple reflection of sexual maturity. While the brush bulls will rub trees, spar with other bulls, and really get into the bugling scene, spikes are reluctant to take part in any of these activities.

They spend their summers with the cows, not with the other bulls that will be sparring once their antlers grow hard in early August. Rather than rubbing their antlers with vigor on trees or ripping up saplings with them, some spikes shed their velvet late or don't shed it at all. And their voices are apt to be squeaky, immature, and untested, compared to the full bugles of the bigger bulls.

Without the company of cows to help protect them, these spikes are extremely vulnerable to the hunter. They're gullible. They're confused. They make plenty of mistakes. And they often even give a hunter multiple chances at them, if a bullet or arrow doesn't hit them the first time.

The primary tool of the hunter who wants to take a spike is the cow call. In fact, it's really all you need.

A bull call, on the other hand, might work, but is far less reliable at the task. Because the spikes are basically non-aggressive, it's not likely that they'll come in to take on another bull. The only reason a spike would come in to bull talk, would be to investigate the sound.

Vince Yannone, of Helena, and I used his bugling to lure in one such spike a few seasons back. It was archery season in a remote section of the mountains when Yannone got the initial, squealing reply to his grunts and bugles. Moving in closer, he bugled again and the spike came in silently. The spike measured its pace carefully, kept craning its neck to see through the timber, and finally presented itself for a shot. Unfortunately, I sent a thirty-five-yard arrow at this forty-five-yard elk, and my broadhead fell to the ground right at its feet. But rather than running off, Yannone's bugle kept it circling. We never did get the elk, but his curiosity throughout the incident was obvious.

Because of that curiosity and the spikes' desire for company of any kind, a cow call is much more effective in pulling them in. These elk are not as smart as their older brethren, and not as trusting of their own senses as being their first line of defense. As a result, they're easily fooled by the cow call, even when they should know better.

Keith Wheat, Bill Hoppe and I had just jumped a cow and calf on a high mountain hunt when a spike showed just how foolish his age class can be. We could still see the two elk as we lay on top of a little ridge, so I cow called to them and they stopped. The elk were interested in our calling and we were simply watching them, when Hoppe whispered that he heard something behind our backs. We couldn't see over the ridge behind us, but could hear an elk walking not far away. Peeking up over the edge, there was the spike, not ten feet away. When it spotted us, it took off at a dead run. But when I made a cow call, the spike stopped at forty yards, turned, and started coming back. He hung around for quite a while before leaving for good, trying his hardest to transform our man shapes into the elk which seemed to be calling to him.

On another occasion, Russ Laubach was adjusting the rubber bands and blowing on his cow call with two of his hunting partners when a calf and later a spike came in. As the spike closed to within fifty yards, Laubach took a shot and missed when the lower limb of his bow hit his leg. The bull ran off to three hundred yards, but was lured back by cow calls to the same spot fifty yards away. The hunter's second arrow went over the spike's back, spooking him again.

Bull Talk

Spikes are the babes of the woods looking for any company they can find.
Ron Shade photo.

After that, Laubach figured his chances were over and he began concentrating on a big herd of elk that emerged a half-mile away. Blowing his cow call intermittently, all eyes were on that herd of elk. So it came as a bit of a surprise when Laubach turned around to see the spike once more, directly downwind from him, just thirty yards away. When the spike spotted him that time, he ran off for good. But the yearling bull had come in to the call three times, and had two arrows sent in his direction, before he finally figured out that all was not as it appeared.

With the cow call, instances like this aren't as rare as you might imagine. Not only do the elk lack experience at detecting danger, their very nature makes them want to believe, rather than be suspicious, of cow sounds. Off on their own, they want the company of other elk and the come-over-here, everything-is-fine language of cow talk suits them well. In terms of responding to cow talk, they come in more readily than any other class of elk.

If there's a problem with spikes, it may be that they're too vulnerable to the hunter under too many circumstances. As a result, some states like Montana, have adopted branch-antlered-only bull regulations in certain districts to try to offer the yearlings a little protection during their first hunting season alone. The reason for that regulation is that too many spikes were being killed too easily. They made up too great a percentage of the total kill and not enough of them were getting a chance to become branch-antlered bulls. If the spikes had another year of experience behind them, they might have a better chance at survival as two-year-olds to become the truly big bulls of the future.

Whether that move toward helping the trophy bull situation will work out in the end, only time will tell. One thing is certain, however. Spikes are highly vulnerable to the caller all through autumn. They make up the bulk of the bull kill wherever they're legal game. And they are among the most prized of the elk for the experienced hunter who knows what he's looking for in prime table fare. Right behind a fat, dry cow, a spike bull offers the next sure bet for tasty and tender meat.

In rifle season, they're easy to pull within range. And even in archery situations, they often come in close enough for a shot. These five-hundred-pound babes of the woods are just too infatuated with the cow talk not to give the hunter an opportunity. They want friendship wherever they can find it. So if you get nervous and miss your shot at them the first time, cow call back at them again. They just might be friendly enough to give you another shot.

When, Where, and How

There's no exact recipe for successfully calling in a bull elk. It's not that much of a science. And in terms of skill, it's only part of the complete picture.

Rather, good elk callers are a little more like a-dash-of this-a-dash-of-that cooks, seat-of-the-pants fliers, or play-it-by-ear musicians. They get a feel for elk calling. They react to the situation at the time, then use their experience to tell them what sound to make next.

This makes it awfully tough to prescribe a calling sequence for you that's going to work every time you get close to a bull. Some tactics work one time and fail the next. Some are tried and true, but need a little extra boost from time to time to pull in a bull. And then, there are some bulls which are destined to come in no matter how good or bad your calling may be.

There are some tendencies, however, and some hints to making you a better caller. You have to know when to call. You have to know where. And if you get both of those factors figured out, then you can worry about how to call effectively.

When and where are the two most important cornerstones of this elk calling triangle. It does you no good to call in the feeding grounds at the middle of the day, when the elk are in their beds. It's just as bad to work near the bedding grounds in the early morning, before the elk are there. By understanding the herd's daily routine, you can get a better feel for where you should be and when you should be there.

In terms of when bulls are most actively calling, they are undeniably the most vocal at night, when they're on the feeding grounds. Early morning tactics dictate that the hunter be near those areas if he hopes to get an answer to his call. By mid-morning, at the latest, the elk should be in their bedding grounds. But there's a quiet time here, during the late morning hours, when the bulls don't seem very willing to respond. They rest and digest their food, sleeping off the activities of the night before. Then, around noon and into the afternoon, they begin becoming more responsive again. You may not hear much bugling during those hours, but you can lure a bull out of a bedding area. As the setting sun starts to lengthen the shadows again, the elk get increasingly active. They're up and around, getting ready to return to their feeding areas. As they get more active, the bugling begins in earnest again. That time period, too, is a good opportunity to be working your call.

In terms of how to make elk talk, the sounds themselves break down into four basic calls, with as many modifications as a hunter wishes to make. The first of those sounds is the calf call, a one-second, high-pitched mixture of a chirp and mewing sound. The second is a cow call, a two-second version of the same thing, which is slightly deeper in tone. The third is the bull squeal, a high-pitched, pretty-much single-note, nasal whistle. Finally, there is the full bugle, which incorporates a rising, extended squeal with a series of grunts on the end to imitate a bull.

Everything else is simply a variation on these four themes. It may be that one elk caller prefers to make a raspy bugle which sounds almost like an elk screaming or roaring, rather than the more melodic, pure-note bugle. In terms of sequence, it's possible that one hunter squeals, bugles, then squeals again. All that is a matter of individual style, what has worked for the hunter before,

Work them right and you can get real close like the camouflaged hunter at lower left. Ron Shade photo.

or what he feels will work at that particular point in time, with that particular bull.

What we're going to talk about here are some basic tendencies for elk calling which will work under most circumstances, as well as some basic pitfalls that hunters should avoid. Foremost among those pitfalls is the hunter's reliance on the full bugle to get the job done.

Listen carefully the next time you hear your partner or some other hunter in the mountains trying to call in an elk with a full bugle. What you'll find is that the grunts at the end of his calling are what separate the good callers from the bad. And believe me, the bad far outnumber the good. Most hunters can master the squeal with many of the bull calls on the market. What they have trouble with are the grunts. For some reason, no matter what brand call a hunter is using, the grunts are the most difficult part of elk calling to master. And if you can pick out the good from the bad and the real elk from the hunters, you can bet that a bull is able to do the same thing.

The good news about grunts, however, is that they really aren't all that critical to elk calling success. One of the basic truths of elk calling is that a hunter makes the squeals for the elk, while he makes the grunts for himself. It comes down to a matter of personal pride and calling skill that a hunter makes his grunts. As far as the bulls are concerned, the grunts really aren't necessary and may, in fact, scare away more bulls than they ever bring in.

One of the reasons that people have so much trouble with grunts is that they are blowing into the call incorrectly. They blow with their throats and chests, rather than pushing the air out with their diaphragms and stomachs. By working your diaphragm, that thin wall of muscle between your chest cavity and internal organs, you force the air out through the call in the proper manner. You can punch out the grunts and make them seem realistic. A good way to tell if you're blowing properly, is to simply look at your call. If you're blowing too much from the throat, the call will collect moisture quickly. Using your diaphragm to force out air, your call will be much drier at the end of your calling sequence.

The hunter should remember, however, that the grunts are not that critical to his calling success. The squeal is really the call that a hunter wants to concentrate on as his basic bull talk. Perhaps not surprisingly, this bit of knowledge vindicates all the old-time elk callers who were out in the mountains using those elk whistles. These days, serious elk callers, tend to shake their heads and appear a bit smug when they talk about the old days or meet someone carrying one of those old whistles. Never mind that those elk whistles have called in a lot of bulls over the years. It's just that now, there are so many other elk calls on the market that can mimic the bugle of a bull more exactly. The new calls undoubtedly are more effective in making more realistic elk sounds. Still, those early whistles had the right plan of attack. They hit the bulls with their pet weapon, right where the elk were most vulnerable, in mimicking the squeal.

The squeal call is at its best at the peak of the rut. That's when the bulls will be most active in taking on other bulls. The beauty of the squeal at that time is underscored by the fact it will call in bulls of all sizes. The full bugle might intimidate the single brush bulls and would certainly scare the spikes. It could also be the signal for brush bulls with cows to head them out of the country before the big bull, the one you are imitating with the full bugle, steals them away. The squeal, instead, can be taken for a smaller bull, perhaps one of those brush bulls, which might be ripe for a sparring match or one whose cows can be stolen. It will bring in the herd bulls to drive the intruder off. It will bring in other brush bulls. And it might even pull in an inquisitive spike who will sneak in for a look at the source of the squealing.

The full bugle, on the other hand, is perhaps most effective as a locating call. It can be blown loudly, from the low pitch that starts it, through the squeal and on to a series of grunts just for practice, to find out if there are any elk in the drainage. What you are imitating is the bugles that a hunter is likely to hear bulls make from far away. It carries well in the open and can trigger responses from a great distance.

The full bugle, however, should be used judiciously with squeals and cow talk while you're actually talking to a bull. It's the type of call that can begin to heat up a bull, who might not be quite hot enough yet to come into close range. It's also the sound you need to enrage a bull that's already coming and speaking your language. But it shouldn't be used alone. Its chances for success as the hunter's lone brand of elk talk aren't really all that good unless the bull is so hot he'll come under any circumstances. Unfortunately, the full bugle is the one you most commonly hear

The old-time elk whistles were on the right track to imitate a bull squeal.
Gary Swanson photo.

being made by other hunters. But in truth, it's more like a fine wine that should be sipped rather than guzzled. Use it carefully, and at the right time, and the full bugle will work for you. Use it too much and you may drive away far more elk than you ever call in.

As far as the cow and calf sounds are concerned, think of them as the liberally-applied cement that sticks your whole calling sequence together. They are both the teasers and the masks for everything else you do. On their own, they can entice a bull because they give the impression there are cows in the neighborhood that can be stolen away by anyone tough enough to take them. The cow and calf sounds also give the impression that all is well in the elk world. This all-is-well aspect can be vital to covering mistakes.

If you make a sour note with the bull call, go to the cow call to cover the mistake. If a bull suddenly turns off and won't answer, go to the cow call to get him started back up again. If you are biding your time, trying to get in sync with a bull's own bugling, go to the cow call. By making cow and calf sounds the foundation of your calling, you can lure in many bulls that would otherwise head out for parts unknown, the way they do for hunters who stick strictly with the bull call.

These four calls aren't the only sounds that elk make, of course. There are many other noises that come from elk, too. I've heard them grunt and snort almost like a pig. They squeal in little short gasps. They roar and scream and grind their teeth. And there are hunters who have mastered the entire elk vocabulary, much the same way expert waterfowl or turkey hunters can talk the vernacular of their chosen species.

In elk hunting, however, the calf call, cow call, bull squeal, and full bugle, are really all the language you need to know. Used in the right combination, they will effectively bring in a bull just as long as you remember that this is only one point of the calling triangle. When and where are the other two, the ones that are even more important. Without being where the elk are, when they are to be found there, how you call really makes no difference at all.

Overbugling and Underbugling

Act and react is the name of the game when talking to elk at the peak of the rut. There are times to initiate the conversation with a bull, and times to let the bull do the talking. Unfortunately, all of this is pretty much what comes naturally to you. You play it by ear as you go.

If there's one guideline to calling in a bull at this time of year, it's to let the bull set the tone for your conversation. Just follow his lead, tend more toward squeals than full bugles, and mix in calf and cow calls liberally along the way. Do that and you have as good a chance as anyone to pull a bull within shooting range.

The basic sin that most hunters make at the peak of the rut is underbugling. For one thing, they can't believe a bull could be that talkative. For another, they have doubts about their own skills. Perhaps that's because many of us are unexplainably embarrassed by the way we sound. We'll toot away on our calls during those drives to and from work. We'll squeeze in a little practice at home, when the wife and kids are away. We'll even try a few toots in the backyard much to the dismay of the people living on the next block. Yet we're somehow fearful of letting an elk hear us. We're afraid that the elk might think we're a bunch of amateurs. We're afraid of four, five, and six-point rejection and alienation of affection by entire herds of cows.

The good news is that it's awfully tough to overbugle at the peak of the rut. This is especially true if you use calf and cow talk. And even with your squeals and bugles, it's not likely that a bull will mind, as long as you're making good elk music.

To give you an example of calling sequences and how they work on elk, I taped the responses of a herd bull over several five-minute spans. The whole thing began at about 1 p.m. on a sunny day at the peak of the rut. But this time, I wasn't hunting for the herd bull. I had filled my tag earlier in the season and simply wanted to get a guage on just what my calling sequence would be and how he would respond. The chart follows to show my calling frequency, the type of calls I used, and just how often the herd bull responded.

There are some things you should know to explain this chart a little further. For one thing, I never pressured the bull as I would have had I been hunting for him. I held my position and just kept on calling. Had I wanted the herd bull, it wouldn't have been very tough to get close to him.

The bull was working his herd of cows in the timber all the while I was talking to him. And he had plenty of competition to worry

First Five Minutes of Calling a Herd Bull

— FIRST 60 SECONDS —

MY CALLING					
10 sec.	20 sec.	30 sec.	40 sec.	50 sec.	60 sec.
c cc	b bbB	c cc	b bB	ccC	bB

BULL ANSWERING					
10 sec.	20 sec.	30 sec.	40 sec.	50 sec.	60 sec.
X	X	X X		X	X

— SECOND 60 SECONDS —

MY CALLING					
10 sec.	20 sec.	30 sec.	40 sec.	50 sec.	60 sec.
bB	c c	bb	bB	b	bB

BULL ANSWERING					
10 sec.	20 sec.	30 sec.	40 sec.	50 sec.	60 sec.
XX		X	X	X X	X

— THIRD 60 SECONDS —

MY CALLING					
10 sec.	20 sec.	30 sec.	40 sec.	50 sec.	60 sec.
	b b b	bB cc	ccC	bB	B

BULL ANSWERING					
10 sec.	20 sec.	30 sec.	40 sec.	50 sec.	60 sec.
X X		X X		X	X

— FOURTH 60 SECONDS —

MY CALLING					
10 sec.	20 sec.	30 sec.	40 sec.	50 sec.	60 sec.
bb c	ccC	bB		b	b

BULL ANSWERING					
10 sec.	20 sec.	30 sec.	40 sec.	50 sec.	60 sec.
				XX	

— FIFTH 60 SECONDS —

MY CALLING					
10 sec.	20 sec.	30 sec.	40 sec.	50 sec.	60 sec.
b cc	c		bB		bbb cc

BULL ANSWERING					
10 sec.	20 sec.	30 sec.	40 sec.	50 sec.	60 sec.
				X	X

CODE: c = CALF CALL, C = COW CALL,
b = BULL SQUEAL CALL, B = BULL CALL WITH GRUNTS
X = HERD BULL ANSWERING

about. The area had been silent when I first arrived, but after the herd bull and I went back and forth for a while, it came alive with elk. There were satellite bulls chiming in from all over the timbered slopes and other bulls seemed to be coming in.

All I kept track of for the chart, was the answers of the herd bull as he worked his herd and tried to keep the satellite bulls at bay at the other end of his harem.

If you noticed that the number of answers the bull came back with tailed off in the final two minutes, it's because he came out into the clear during that time to look me over. With a rifle and a tag in my pocket, it would have been one dead herd bull. When he came out to look for the source of the elk sounds I was making, he saw nothing. As a result, he concentrated his efforts on the other end of the herd where he could see the brush bulls that were talking to him.

Had I been serious about getting within bow range of him, I would have gotten closer to my end of the herd, then made my calls from there. The way to do it would have been to move in when he went to the other end of the herd. That way, I would have been waiting for him when he came back. He would have had to come over, to investigate the calf and cow sounds so close to his herd, or to drive off the other bull. That would have been my chance to get him within spitting distance or bow range, which-ever was closer.

Just because the herd bull didn't come that close to my calling position doesn't mean that I couldn't have had a bull with my bow during this episode either. During the time I was calling, two different bulls came within bow range. One was a brush bull that came in quickly and then ran off. The other was a silent bull, a good six-point, that snuck in close and then moved away.

I don't know how many satellite bulls there were to that elk herd, but there were more than a few. At times, it's a little hard to tell, because the bulls will move around between bugles. Because of their numbers, it's not uncommon to have those bulls coming in whenever you're working a herd. It's also not uncommon to have a brush bull rush in and rush away from your calling. But just because a brush bull runs off, that doesn't mean the herd is spooked and all is lost. Instead, this simply shows the nature of the brush bulls which are satellites to the herd. They are young and impetuous. They run all over the place in the rut.

When talking to bulls at the peak of the rut, it's almost impossible to call too much. Michael Sample photo.

So if one comes in and leaves, your hunting success may still be secure. Those bulls are simply playing out their roles and another brush bull could appear at any moment. If you spook the cows out of the country, however, that's the time to begin worrying, because they have likely taken the herd bull and satellites with them.

Don't hold back because the bulls seem to respond best the louder you call. Ron Shade photo.

The main thing for the hunter to have is patience when working on a herd. If you have the herd bull answering and have the satellites working the herd, you're in a good position to get some action. If the herd bull doesn't come in, perhaps a silent bull or one of the brush bulls will make an appearance.

To understand just how active they can be, you have to look no further than the incident I've been describing. The calling sequence just relates the first five minutes of my conversation with the herd bull. The actual calling went on for forty-five minutes. In that time, I would have had a second crack at the herd bull with a rifle. That forty-five minutes of activity also lured in other bulls from the area which would have been fair game.

And in the end, the herd bull was just about as hot as he was at the start. During the first five minutes, he bugled twenty-three times. In the last five minutes of calling, he still answered me twenty-three times.

If you think this might be an isolated incident, you should know that I pulled off the same thing, with the same tape recorder, two days later, and about fifty miles away from the first calling site. This time, it was a herd bull and about forty cows. In the first five minutes, he answered me nineteen times. After twenty minutes, a silent bull came within thirty yards of me. Another brush bull came in as well and the herd bull would have died many times had I been hunting with a rifle. Just to test if the herd bull could be worked over again, I quit for about thirty minutes and the bugling died out. Starting my sequence again, the herd bull responded twenty-three times in five minutes. Fifteen minutes later, he bugled twenty-three times again in a five-minute span.

That's a lot of bugling, much more than many hunters would expect in such a short span of time. But it reflects just how hot those bulls can get at the peak of the rut. And it also tells a hunter that he should be aggressive in his calling. This is the time to patiently press those bulls. It's the time that you can get them hot enough that they'll make mistakes. And the more calling you do, and the more bugling the herd bull does, the better your chances at bringing in some of the other bulls that might be in the area.

To test this overbugling-underbugling theory a bit more, I went into elk-rich Yellowstone National Park armed with one of those portable tape players fitted with a loudspeaker. This was back in the days before people frowned on working over the Park elk with calls. Since then, the bugling season has become a hot tourist time in Yellowstone, just because of the show the elk put on. And with so many people packing elk calls, I can agree with the new feeling on calls there.

Back when I had my speaker-recorder, the tape I was using played elk bugles over and over and over again. It was pretty much nonstop bull calls for as long as the tape ran. The question was, should I turn the recorder off after the first few bugles and wait, then turn it on again? Should I play it at full volume or more quietly? After experimenting for three days, I found out that full volume and letting it play continuously seemed to work the best.

In three days' time with that routine, I called in twenty-seven bulls with that recorder. I called in five bulls at one time. I had one bull pass within fifteen steps of me and not pay any attention, even though I was standing right out in the open. It walked up to the recorder and pointed it like a bird dog. Then it turned around and ran off, but came back right to the same spot. He knew it wasn't an elk. He knew that something wasn't right. But he just couldn't stay away.

What the experiment told me was that you couldn't bugle too loudly. You couldn't really bugle too much, either. It brought the elk in better and faster than bugling spasmodically. Since that time, I've added that concept to my own calling and filled the mountains with elk music.

You can't really overbugle during the peak of the rut. Before the peak and after the peak, that may be different. During those times, the cow and calf calls and a few squeals might work better. But during that peak, don't hold back. Bugle and squeal and cow call and calf call as hard as you want. Do it as loud as you want. Do it as often as you want. This is the time to make all that calling in your car and your home pay off. And don't feel embarrassed about it either. If you did your homework with all that practice, you've earned your right to hit the high country and make a little noise.

Sunny, Cloudy, Uphill, and Down

Elk hunters who hope to call in a bull, face a world full of variables during the height of the rut. Most often, these variables are not under their control. You can't put a bull right where you want him. You can't count on the time of day when you'll run into him. And we all know, you can't predict the weather that's going to hit when you plan your hunting trip far in advance.

There was a week-long pack trip into the big bull country of Montana's Bob Marshall Wilderness, for example, at what we figured would be the peak of the rut. Instead, we had six straight days of soggy September snow, which turned off the bugling activity almost completely. We could do little but hope for a break in the weather, but that didn't arrive until the day before we had to head back out of the wilderness. The bulls sang loud and long that last day, but by then, the bulk of our hunting time was gone. We never got a bull. Pinning your hopes on just one good day usually isn't enough to get the job done.

Given a choice we never seem to have, elk hunters would opt for sunny days, cold nights, and crisp, calm mornings. Those are the types of days that seem to get the juices flowing in bull elk, just as beautiful autumn days get them flowing in the hunters who go after those bulls. The bulls seem to bugle more and respond better to calling when the weather is good.

That doesn't mean that bulls won't come in under other weather conditions. Even in that week of snow, our hunting party had bulls answering. But they seemed to be more reluctant than if the weather had been better. They answered weakly and never did come in. Each time the weather tried to break, however, the bulls would get more active as if in anticipation of the long-awaited sun. There was a spot of sun late one evening, for example, and the whole drainage we were working seemed to come to life. And on that last afternoon, when the skies cleared, there were elk walking and talking all around us.

All a hunter can do is stick with his calling plans, no matter what weather conditions mother nature throws at him. Calling strategies remain basically the same in any weather. You just have to work a little harder when the weather turns sour. But the elk will basically be found in the same places. Work the feeding areas in the early morning. Catch them on the travel routes later in the morning. And try to lure them out of the wallows and bedding areas in the afternoon.

When you get to an area where you figure there are elk, get out your cow and bull calls and work them. Wait there twenty or thirty minutes after you make your calls, even if you don't hear any responses, then move on. That's the way to locate elk. If you find no takers, a hunter should move about four-hundred or five-hundred yards and repeat the process.

If you've done your scouting, you know the places the elk are likely to be found. That scouting and knowledge of the area is your key to success no matter what the weather. If you're calling in the early morning, you're going to call from the bottoms where they feed. Later in the day, you should be higher on the mountain. You know where the wallows are located from your scouting, and you do your calling there around noon. Perhaps in the early afternoon, you move on to the bedding areas and use your cow talk more than your bull talk in hopes of luring elk out of their beds or heating up a bull.

One of the problems a hunter faces in working the wallows and near bedding areas is that despite the fact the elk are there, they don't always answer you. If you don't get an answer, that may mean you're in those places at the wrong time. Perhaps they're not ready to answer you. If they have just arrived in the bedding area from a night of feeding and running around, they often rest for a time and no amount of calling will awaken them to action.

If a bull does answer, it's time to work him in earnest, adopting the posture of aggression that seems to work best at the peak of the rut. Move in on him and try to get either above, or at the same level, as the elk you're talking to. It's much easier to bring a bull up the mountainside to you or to get him to move at the same level. For some reason, they are more hesitant to go down to a caller.

Even if you get in the right position to call, however, the bull may decide not to cooperate. He may head out on you. He may not budge from his position. He may come in a distance, then stop to work over a tree with his antlers, to assess the situation, or just to keep a safe distance. Or, he may charge right in.

Elk are much like people in their reactions to particular situations. They all have different personalities. The appropriate response for one bull may be far different from another. That's why it can be so frustrating to decide the course of action a hunter should take next.

The rule of thumb, at the peak of the rut especially, is to press the bull. Move in as close as you dare, to force his hand and make him do something. Blow your calls often. Try to get him heated

Given the choice, a hunter should hope for warm, clear days and crisp, cold nights. Mark Henckel photo.

up. Even in the early afternoon, it's possible to get a herd bull red-hot and ready. And you can just as easily pull the satellites right out of their beds.

You have to be aggressive, go after him, and talk to him in his own language. If he squeals at you, squeal back at him. If he goes into a full bugle, give him a full bugle back. Imitating their sounds seems to get them going. And, based on my own experiences, I feel the imitation of sounds goes both ways. I've had bulls come right back with the same sounds I was making. What you want to do is heat up the exchanges between you and the bull. You want to make the bull defend his position. If you can get them going, a hot bull can be the easiest of elk to bring in to the call. If you only get them hot enough, virtually anything will work on bringing them in, from a spent rifle shell to the most expensive of calls.

If there's a problem with this aggressive stance, it's that if you move in too close to the bull, you might spook his cows. Spook them and they'll head out of the country with the bulls in tow. Also, if you don't show some patience, you may agitate the bull before he's ready to come to you. If you upset him before he's ready, he may head his cows out of there, too.

One plan of attack to get around these problems is to hunt with a partner. Teamwork can do a great deal to enhance the chances of you or your buddy taking a bull.

One key piece of information to remember in an elk calling situation is that the bull is going to be keying in on the caller. By making his sounds, the caller is telegraphing his exact location to the bull at all times. That leaves the other hunter, the non-caller, free to sneak around and do some damage.

When the two of you move in on a bugling bull, put the non-caller out in front about fifty yards. Let the non-caller set the pace of your movements while the caller concentrates on working the bull. The non-caller can concentrate on looking for the bull, moving slowly through the timber while keeping low to the ground. Many times, this strategy pays off. Sometimes, for example, a bull will only come in to within sixty yards of the caller. If that's the case, the non-caller has a ten-yard shot.

Sometimes, two hunters can also pull in a bull with a well-executed retreat. If the bull comes in close, but not close enough, and then won't come any closer, have the caller pull back while

A hunter should be aggressive in working a herd bull to force the elk to make a move. Michael Sample photo.

the non-caller holds his ground. That retreat can sometimes get the bull coming again and trick him into walking right into the non-caller's sights.

A friend, Rob Seelye, of Laurel, used the buddy system another way. He and his partner were hunting with some other friends in an area where they knew there were elk, but couldn't get any responses to their bugles. Seelye and his partner, Dan Moore of Kalispell, moved apart a distance, then started answering each other's bugles. Before they knew it, their bugling back and forth had heated up the bulls they knew were in the area. Their group ended up taking two five-point bulls with their bows, at fifteen and twenty yards, in what had been a silent drainage before their double bugling strategy paid off.

Two callers can also work the cow call more effectively than just one caller. With two callers mixing their cow and calf sounds, it can make it appear as if a whole herd of elk has just moved into the area.

If there's a problem with trying to prescribe exact answers to elk hunting situations, however, it goes back to what we said at the start. Almost every incident is frought with variables. You may not be able to get uphill of the bull and work down on him. You may not know the exact path an elk will be using so that your partner can get an open shot. You may not be able to wait for a sunny, calm day if your vacation is set during the time the equinox storms hit the high country. And you may not be able to hunt with a partner every time you take to the mountains.

All I can give you is some tendencies of the elk and some experiences of my own. Hopefully, those tendencies and stories can help prepare you for the situations you will encounter on your own hunting trips. For the fine details on particular instances, you have to get out there and cope with them for yourself.

Given the choice, however, I always go for the sunny, uphill, partner, and plenty of elk. If you can only be at the right place, at the right time, to find plenty of elk, many of the other problems presented by variables will be solved. Even though you can only hang your tag on one of them, it makes it a lot easier to find that lone animal if there are a lot of elk around to increase your chances. Who knows, if you can only find enough elk, you might even take one on a cloudy day, heading downhill, in a blinding blizzard, with a stiff wind blowing, and while you're hunting alone. Some folks in elk country do just that every year.

The Silent Bull

It was rapidly shaping up as yet another elk hunting disaster. And it wasn't a very pretty day to be courting disaster, either. After getting some answers from a good bull while calling from the ridgetop, my bugling elk was now heading out across the basin. With his passing, any warmth he brought to a wind-blown, rain-spattered day, was rapidly drowning in the cold mist.

There was little to do but go after him. The only strategy I had left was to cover ground quickly, bugle just often enough to keep track of him, and hope to either pressure him into turning back or figure out his exit route from the basin and head him off at the pass. I crossed the clearing and hit the timber at a brisk walk, ended up dodging two mule deer does who watched carefully as I passed, then struck a trail on the sideslope that went in the bull's general direction.

But with each new blast from my elk whistle, the bull was getting further and further away. At least, he was still hot. My calls received instant answers. Once, even when I was too winded to build up air pressure to make the three-note whistle produce more than a single note, he still answered back.

All hope of ever catching him, however, appeared to be lost when I noticed a movement up the slope to my right and behind me. It was a second bull with his neck outstretched scanning for a glimpse of the bugling bull I was imitating. His coat was matted with rain and his six-by-five rack was glistening in the dim light of the timber. Just forty yards away when I first spotted him, he was walking along a trail that would make him pass within twenty-five yards of me. As I knelt and nocked an arrow, he continued his stalk, passing behind a tree as I came to full-draw. Then he stopped behind some thin brush, just short of an open shot. I tried the shot anyway but the arrow deflected wide in front of him. Then he made his fatal mistake. The bull made one more forward step into the clear and turned, looking down the slope toward me. A second arrow at twenty-four paces went up through his chest and buried in his spine, dropping him in his tracks.

It was my first brush with a silent bull and one that made the cold chill of that late September day seem more like bluebirds

Silent bulls are the heirs-apparent to the herd masters who know enough to keep quiet. Bob Zellar photo.

and sunshine. That it took us two days to get the bull out of there hardly mattered. It was a good bull, a clean kill, and an incident that would provide a premonition of much elk hunting in the future.

If there's a new wave of elk in the woods that hunters should be aware of, it is the silent bull. Not that there haven't always been some of them around.

In the past, these silent bulls tended to be the in-between class of mature bulls. They were bigger than the raghorns and brush bulls. But they fell short of the true herd masters. These were good bulls who were pretenders to the throne and already discovered that there were benefits to holding their tongue.

While the smaller brush bulls sounded off their positions and made brash moves at the herd bulls, the silent bulls actually had a chance at cutting loose a cow or two if they just played it sneaky. Given a year or two more age and stature, they might even get big enough to command harems of their own. But right now, they

As more hunters have tried their luck with a call, elk have grown more silent and wary. Mark Henckel photo.

either knew when they were overmatched by the bigger bulls or perhaps they had just been whipped in a fight for control. But given the guile of their years in the woods, they might pick up a cow or two of their own if they shadowed the herd and struck when the old man was off chasing the youngsters who didn't know enough to keep quiet.

In a word, these bulls are non-aggressive. They're interested in the action, but not interested enough to lend their voices or spoil for a fight. But just because they're non-aggressive, that doesn't mean that they're not good bulls. Just the opposite is true. Often they are good, solid six-points who might not be big enough to make the record book, but are certainly good enough for a winter's worth of bragging to your friends. They just fall a bit short of the herd bulls in stature and are awaiting their chance at the throne.

That more traditional view of the silent bull has changed somewhat in recent years, however. Bulls of almost any size can be silent bulls now. This phenomenon has come about as a result of hunting. Elk calling has become more widespread during the past few decades. Good callers and bad have made elk more wary of making noise, even at the peak of the rut. Elk that inhabit country where there are likely to be a lot of hunters are becoming increasingly silent. In some parts of the Rockies, in fact, hunters swear that elk don't bugle at all.

As a result, it's not enough for hunters who have tuned their ears to listen for the bugles of distant bulls. They have to have their eyes peeled for bulls that might be sneaking in around them, too.

Much of the blame for bulls stopping bugling has been centered around hunters using elk whistles and bull calls of all descriptions. Either the notes they were making were bad in the first place and the elk noticed they were phonies. Or, the elk were called in and spooked by someone using a bull call. While elk aren't necessarily geniuses, they do know when it's time to shut up. If they know there are hunters in the neighborhood by the calls they are making, they're going to play it cagey. If they've been fooled by a Brand X call or Brand Z whistle, they're going to remember that, too.

In any event, they're going to be silent. They're going to silently sneak away. Or, if the bull call is good enough, they're going to silently come in for a look. And, if we're talking about the traditional non-aggressive bull, he may not leave or come in. Just be silent and hold their ground at a safe distance until the time is right to make a move.

All that has changed somewhat with the more widespread use of the cow call, however. Because the presence of cows presents no challenge, yet may offer the possibilities of one coming into heat, the rules of the game have been changed for both the silent-aggressive and non-aggressive bulls. A lone cow in the timber is an opportunity, not something to be afraid of.

Some hunters have had their nerves jangled unwittingly by this change of events. More than a few have talked about sitting on a log far back in the timber tuning and practicitng their cow calls, only to have a bull sneak in on them. In most instances, these bulls did more to precipitate heart attacks than good arrows or bullets sent in their direction.

If you can picture it, imagine a dead quiet patch of timber and a man completely off-guard tooting on his call. Then put a bull in the picture, say, about twenty yards away. Then have the bull bugle at the man at full volume. No one has admitted to mixing his urine scents in situations like these. But, then again, it hasn't happened to me yet.

The lesson in all this is that the cow calls do work well on the silent bulls. And, for their part, hunters have to be ready for them. What makes silent bulls so tough is that the hunter has no idea what direction they are coming from. The only sure bet is that the silent bulls probably won't be walking in the hunter's own tracks because the bull will smell him if he comes in that way. But any other direction is fair game.

Where allowed, a good set of camouflage clothing with a face mask or face paint and gloves will definitely help the hunter in his quest for silent bulls. That clothing will help cover his movements and, by walking low to the ground, his outline will be less obvious to the searching eyes of the bull.

But there really isn't much more advice that will help a hunter except to keep his eyes peeled for movements, his ears tuned for the step of a sneaking elk, and his nose clear in hopes of catching a whiff of elk scent.

The silent bull, I'm afraid, is always going to be a tough customer for the hunter. Just as the hunter sneaks through elk country looking for bulls, the bulls are sneaking through elk country looking for bulls, cows, and hunters. The only solace in this whole chain of events is that the hunter of the future can expect to get plenty of practice in working silent bulls. They're a part of the elk world that's definitely on the rise. Yet they're a part that's well worth the hunter's time in getting to know on an intimate basis.

The Gang's All Here

Okay, so you got your wish. You wanted to call in some elk and get a little action on your hunting trip. Now, you've got more action than you ever wanted. And more elk, too.

There are elk to the right of you. There are elk to the left of you. There are elk still coming in. And, somewhere in the middle of this elk invasion, is the bull of your dreams. If you can only find him, and then get a shot at him, you'll have it made.

Although it should sound like a hunter's dream, finding yourself in the middle of an elk herd can be a nightmare. Perhaps it's nature's way of punishing the greedy. You spent your whole summer dreaming about being awash in elk. You neglected your family to go on scouting trips. You assaulted their ears with your constant bugling. You spent all those hours at the practice range instead of weeding the garden, cutting the lawn, and pruning the hedge. And, finally, you talked about taking a bull so much that you actually started sprouting antlers yourself. Well you've got them, buster, you've got them all. Now, what are you going to do with them?

Greed is one of the larger sins that can affect an elk hunter, especially one that hunts in the rut. You get yourself worked up to the point that your expectations become bigger than life. Cows aren't worthy of your attention. Spike bulls are trivial. And even brush bulls begin to appear sickly as a hunter's imagination begins to get carried away. This happens easily, but nature has a way of getting even and snapping a hunter back to reality in a hurry.

Rod Churchwell and I were set up for a weekend hunting trip which put just those kind of visions in our head. We were camped in the rain and had just turned in when the elk invasion began. They moved in near our campsite and bugled all night long. With the sounds of bulls bugling here and bulls bugling there, it was easy for imaginations to run away with themselves.

We awakened before dawn, ate a cold breakfast, and started out in the direction they had been bugling. But by the time daylight

If you bring in a bull with his harem, there are more eyes that can spot you. Michael Sample photo.

arrived, the elk had vanished. The weather had lifted, but the ground was moist enough that we picked up their tracks and followed them quite a distance. After a while we lost the tracks. We kept on searching high bedding areas and every other likely-looking haunt. We never found them in a whole day's looking, not even a loose cow or scrawny spike. And we didn't find them the next day, either. Where they went, we weren't exactly sure. But the pictures we had in our mind's eye of glorious bulls were suddenly snapped back to reality in a hurry.

The same phenomenon often occurs when a herd of elk does come into your call. Hunters are somehow transformed by the visions of taking a big bull. A guy who would have been more than happy to shoot a cow five minutes ago, turns into Doctor Jeckyl's Hyde when the herd arrives. Their eyes get wide. Their breathing gets choppy. And their knees start to knock. Before he knows what has happened, the hunter has blown a sure thing cow, for a maybe, maybe not, crack at a bull.

This is a decision that every hunter has to make. And he has to live with it, whether he succeeds or not. But I have heard of bowhunters who had cows so close to them that they could have reached out and touched them with their bows. Yet they actually leaned out around them to take a chancy shot through the timber at a bull barely within range. To some hunters, that's a shot well worth taking. To others, it's stupidity in the nth degree.

The thing a hunter has to realize is that when the whole herd comes in, his problems are multiplied exponentially. Ten elk aren't ten times tougher to handle than one elk, they're fifty or a hundred times as tough. The more elk that come in, the less chance you have of putting something over on them.

The problem is one of too many eyes, too many ears, and too many noses which can detect the hunter. And once the first elk makes you out, you have problems. The thing a hunter has to worry most about is the elk seeing you. Unlike bears, which rely heavily on their noses for primary identification of danger, elk seem to use their noses more to verify what their eyes have seen. As a result, it's not advisable that a hunter allow himself to be winded by elk, but he might get away with it. It might make the elk edgy. But, often the elk won't bolt when they get their first whiff.

Hearing is used the same way. Elk are accustomed to hearing some noises in the mountains. They'll use this sense, too, as a secondary line of defense to their eyes. It merely tells them where to look. The elk's next step is to see if he can spot the hunter. Once the hunter is spotted, this is the time he hears that horrible bark. The whole herd is likely to take off as if shot out of a cannon. That warning bark, in fact, seems to be a message to other elk that, yes, the danger has been spotted and it's time to go.

The hunter who plays it right is going to try to confuse as many elk senses as he can when he gets into a situation like this. He can fool the elk's nose by the proper use of elk scent. He can neutralize the ears by staying quiet. And he can try to avoid their prying eyes by keeping as low to the ground as possible and holding his movements to a minimum. Camouflage clothing, including a headnet or face paint and something to cover the hands, will go a long way toward concealing a hunter. The only thing a hunter has yet to face, is how he's going to go through the movements of drawing his bow or shouldering his rifle. For this, we offer no solutions, except to remember that just because the

When working a herd, it's possible you'll spook the cows who take the bull with them. Ron Shade photo.

bull doesn't see you, that doesn't mean you're home free. The bull is often preoccupied with bugling or hooking his cows. It's those cows which form his primary line of defense. If they spot you and take off, the bull will be gone with them.

The phenomenon of calling in a whole herd isn't generally something that a hunter using a bull call has to worry about. A bull call alone, or even a bull call used in combination with a cow call, isn't going to pull them in. It might lure a bull out of a herd, but not the whole herd. With a cow call alone, however, the whole herd might come in to investigate. In fact, it's not uncommon at all, to bring in herds of ten to fifteen elk with a cow call.

In situations like that, it's likely that the hunter has aroused the interest of the lead cow. And when she comes, all the other elk just tag along.

But we should stress here again, that this is not a desirable situation. Whether they come to you or you go to them, it's far easier to work on a single animal.

In situations when there are many elk around, it's often the ones that a hunter doesn't see that end up ruining his chances. I remember a time, for example, when I was bull calling and got an answer from an elk a half-mile ahead of me in the timber. As

I headed toward him, I called just often enough to keep track of his location until I got within two hundred yards. All that while, the elk hadn't moved.

When I got within one hundred yards, he still hadn't moved. So I kept up my aggressive posture, and kept on moving in his direction. As I got closer, I started crawling and moving more slowly. At that point, I hadn't heard a bugle for quite some time but figured I must have been within about sixty yards of the bull. I let out a squeal on my bull call at that point, but it was just too close. The sound spooked his herd of cows and they took off at a dead run, taking the bull with them.

Another time, I was pulling a similar sneak on a bull, when the cows got the better of me in a different way. Bill Hoppe and I had come in quietly, then split up to move in on a bull we had heard. From my vantage point, I could actually see the tree the elk was rubbing down about a hundred yards away, because he was shaking the tree top. Following the trunk of the tree down with my binoculars, I spotted the bull raking his antlers up and down.

I started mixing my bull and cow calls while Hoppe tried moving in on him, but when I tried to go up the hill a little further to get a better look, there were a dozen cows waiting for me. Scattered through the timber about twenty yards away, they had gathered to investigate the camouflaged form that was making the elk noises. And as soon as I moved, they bolted out of there taking the bull and some other cows with them.

Had we known the herd of elk was that big, we might have worked it differently. But even then, the odds were stacked against us. There are too many eyes, ears, and noses in a herd of elk that big to fool them very often.

So if you're going to have dreams, and visions, and imaginations when it's time to make your big plans, tone them down a bit. It's no picnic to be caught in or by a big herd of elk. Your chances of success will be greater if you wish for something a little more modest and take your chances when they come. But if your heart's still set on that big bull of your dreams and it just can't be swayed, hope and pray, loud and long, that he comes in alone.

■

CALLING TO THE GUN

In much of elk country, the weeks of October and November mean putting away your bows and arrows, donning your blaze orange, and slinging a high-powered rifle over your shoulder.

At this point of autumn, the rut is generally over. The big herd bulls have left the cows, for the most part, to the company of spikes and brush bulls. With this change in elk seasons, the hunter has a new set of rules to follow and new strategies to explore if he's to find success.

While the full bugles that made such beautiful music as they floated over the peaks and valleys have all-but disappeared, that doesn't mean a hunter has to give up calling altogether. Elk can still be fooled by a call, but cow talk is the prescribed language now. But don't think cows will be the only ones listening.

Bulls can be pulled in from a mile away to investigate your cow talk. It can cover your movements in the timber. And it can even stop a bull cold in his tracks so you can shoot at him once, twice, or even more times than that.

This post-rut period, when people are packing more guns than bows and arrows, is also time to think about different hunting strategies. The elk have pulled back into lifestyles that are closer to summer patterns than they are to the peak of the rut. You have to go after them in the heart of their range and be able to read the signs they leave behind to assess how to hunt them.

In short, the rules of elk hunting have changed again. Just as a hunter had to adapt from the pre-rut to the peak of the rut, he has to change again when the post-rut period arrives. If he can successfully make the switch to the post-rut period, he can find an elk in his sights once the gun seasons of late October and November are in full swing.

To Call Or Not To Call

Everybody knows you can't call in an elk during the rifle season, right? In late October and November, the breeding season is over and the bulls aren't bugling. So everyone leaves their calls at home and hunts quietly.

If that's the case, why was Rich Seymour, of Park City, listening in the pre-dawn darkness of opening day to a bull bugling in an open meadow of Montana's Snowcrest Range? It was the third weekend of October last year, well past the peak of the rut. Yet the bull was still working his herd until another group of hunters spooked him out of there before shooting time.

How could John Kremer, who lived in Helena at the time, spend an hour in the third week of October a few years back, watching a six-by-seven bull bugle and work cows? If the peak of the rut was past, breeding still seemed to be on that bull's mind. And he was bugling up a storm.

And how do you explain the record of Ervin Bobo back in the 1959 season? Bobo, of Council, Idaho, had a little help for the hunters he packed back into elk country that fall season. Earlier that year, a cow elk had run into a pole fence at a local airstrip and broke her neck, leaving a bull calf to fend for itself. One of Bobo's friends raised the calf, and that fall, Bobo took it to elk camp with him. To get the bull calf to follow him, he simply fed it chewing tobacco. But Bobo still got the better of the bargain. The calf would call and locate elk for hunters. It turned out to be his best season ever, as fifty-five hunters accounted for forty-two elk. Elk do continue to talk after the rut. By the time the gun hunts are going in earnest, there are still a few bulls bugling, some squealing, and cows and calves speaking their elk language.

In late October, some herd bulls are still with cows and feeling the mating urge. Michael Sample photo.

It's more likely that the influx of hunters during that season does as much to end the heavy bugling time for bulls as the passing of the rut. Elk are more secretive during the rifle seasons of late October and November, simply because they have to be. There are too many hunters packing too many guns for the bulls to be advertising their presence.

As for the rut itself, that, too, may not be entirely over by the time men in orange are stalking the mountain slopes. The breeding season doesn't have the well-defined, tight parameters that hunters like to think it has. It's not confined to the weeks of middle and late September. Some cows come into heat early. Others are late. The bulls remain interested as long as there are cows willing to breed. And some of them, with good memories, may remember the hot times with a herd of cows and be trying to interest them in another fling in the meadow.

As a result, there are some bulls that bugle well into October. Some even let loose with bugles in November and in every other month of the year, too, for that matter. But it's a chancy deal to expect to call one with bull talk in at that time. For one thing, once the mountain states like Montana open their general rifle seasons, I'd be a little afraid of sounding too much like a bull.

Crouching in the brush, making just enough movements to work a call, I'd be worried about having some trigger-happy rifleman convince himself that I was an elk.

But calling still works in the rifle season for the hunter who makes cow talk. The basic urge among elk to be with other elk can still work to the hunter's benefit in late October and November. And no one knows that better than Helena's Vince Yannone.

Yannone has been making cow talk with his throat for years, simply cupping his hands around his mouth and calling. He has been doing that for the better part of two decades. To illustrate how effective it can be, he remembered hunting with Arnold Lyon, a friend from Helena, just a few years ago when his cow talk paid off.

"I called in a nice five-point for Arnold in early November," Yannone said. "He came right to us, but he never made a sound. I called and we waited about fifteen minutes. Some deer came in and then he came walking right in. We backtracked on him and he came in from over a mile away. There was quite a bit of snow and we were able to track him to a point where he was lying with two other animals."

Yannone called in another bull for himself that season, using the method he learned after college, while working as a biologist for the Montana Cooperative Wildlife Research Unit in the early 1970s.

"I've done this off and on and I've had some extremely good luck with it," he said. "On the one I called in for Arnold, they were firing guns all around us and I still brought him in. The majority of the bulls that come in at that time of year come in silent. If they do answer, they don't answer in a bugle. They answer in more of a long bark.

"A lot of people don't think that elk talk except during the rut," Yannone added. "Elk get up and stretch and they'll talk. Although we associate the bugle with the rut, that doesn't mean they won't talk during the rest of the year." What gun hunters seem to forget is that elk do communicate with one another with more than just bugles and squeals. They speak a language that's ingrained in their very being, from the time they're calves at their mother's side until the day they die. In some ways, it's this language that is their true Achilles heel. It makes them vulnerable in the rifle season as well as any other month of the year.

It's only in our hunting of them that this language hasn't been exploited. Generations of big game hunters have developed their autumn traditions, keying in on elk talk only during the rut. Bull talk was the only language those hunters understood. It's our switch to cow talk that has opened up new horizons for them.

Now, those late-autumn, early-winter rifle hunters can join in the calling game. For many of them, it will be their first exposure to calling in elk. And some of them will be understandably dubious about how it could work. After all, there are generations of tradition to be altered here.

It's not necessarily calling under the best conditions, however. I'll grant you that the bulls may not be as receptive as during the pre-rut and peak-of-the-rut periods. While not wanting to get into a numbers game, let's say it works only forty or fifty percent of the time. Even that, however, would mean that a hunter would bring in four or five out of ten bulls in the area that he might not get a look at otherwise. The number of hunters in the mountains, too, could work against a caller at this time of year. Compared to the relatively few hunters afield during the Montana archery season, for example, which coincides with the peak of the rut, the hunts of late October and November are crowded indeed. That number of hunters is bound to make the elk more wary of any action they take at this time of year.

One of the differences in calling strategy between the peak of the rut and this post-rut period is the amount of calling and type of calling that you do. Calf calls, cow calls, and bull squeals are all that are needed during the weeks of late October and November. Full bugles aren't a sound that you want to make. In fact, even the squeal is strictly optional. Rifle hunters who have made the switch to calling consider the calf call to be the most effective during this post-rut period and feel that the timber is the place to be calling. That high-pitched, one-second call will bring in both bulls and cows. Its high pitch travels well in the timber and interests elk of both sexes and all ages.

Another difference between the rut and post-rut is to avoid over-calling. While it's hard to call too loudly or too much at the peak of the rut, it's best to exercise some restraint when calling at this time of year. Position yourself in an area that shows signs of elk use or where you have found elk in the past. Making a few calls,

Some elk will answer back at this time of year, while others may come in silent. Michael Sample photo.

then giving it a long rest to see if something comes in, is a far better way to go. That way, you can listen for elk that might be talking back to you, giving away their position in the process. Or, you can give an elk plenty of opportunity to sneak in silently for a look, the way that five-point bull did for Yannone on his hunt in the snow.

As for making the cow and calf sounds themselves, that's the easy part. All it takes is a call and a little practice. Perhaps the toughest part about calling in elk with a cow call at this time of year is still going to be convincing the hunters to give it a try in the first place. It's going to be difficult to convert someone who has hunted quiet for all his life, to getting out there and making a little elk noise the next time he's in the high country. All we can say is to try it. You'll be pleasantly surprised when you hear the elk talking back to you. And you'll be happier still when you call in your first rifle season bull.

Dead In Their Tracks

Want to share a sinking feeling? Picture yourself on a week-long hunt in the high country. You feel like you've hiked a million miles. Your boots seem to weigh twenty pounds apiece. Your lightweight rifle now weighs a hundred pounds. You've climbed mountain after mountain, explored drainage after drainage, and now your hunting trip is down to its final day.

And there, standing before you through the timber is a good bull elk. He's edgy, though. He knows something is amiss. And you've got to move around one more tree to get a clear shot. It's the moment of truth and the payday for a full week of effort. But if that's the case, who had the horrible sense of humor to put that dry stick under your boot? The boot lands, the stick breaks, and the bull stiffens, stands there for a moment, then bolts off down the mountainside.

This scene of terror is repeated all too often in elk country every season. Over the years, the hunters' screams of anguish have rocked the timber. And the language that those hunters have used are probably the real reason the mountains look blue from a distance. There just wasn't any second chances for hunters who spooked elk by the sounds they made. And if, perish the thought, the hunter had made good on his stalk and missed his shot at the bull, that, too, was the end of the line.

But things have changed a bit in elk country with the advent of the cow call. A hunter can have a second chance, and maybe even a third or fourth, at a spooked elk.

Outfitters in the Gardiner area found out just how valuable the cow and calf sounds could be while guiding hunters who missed their first shots at elk. It was a case of changing their attitudes on traditional hunting methods, however. Like most hunters with something new, they went with their tried and true traditional approach first. The cow call was used only as a last resort.

Bill Hoppe was one of those outfitters who saw the cow call work in amazing fashion on bulls that had been shot at. "The most unique things that have happened with the cow call, and this has happened more than once, are after a hunter has shot at them once or twice or three time, you can still stop them," Hoppe said. "On one occasion, I was able to call an elk back out of a closed area, after it was shot at four times, for the guy to shoot at him again.

"Another time, I had hunters from Big Timber and Miles City who rode into the edge of the timber and rode into three or four bulls. The fellow from Big Timber got off his horse and shot his

A cow call can stop a bull elk cold and allow a hunter to take one or more shots at him. Ron Shade photo.

bull and the other bulls took off running," Hoppe said. "I blew the cow call and by that time, the guy from Miles City got off his horse. He never walked twenty feet and the here are all those bulls. The other three or four had stopped right there. I just kept squealing on the cow call until the other fellow could get in there and get a shot and the other fellow got his elk right there in the same place.

"That's probably the most amazing thing to me. I've used it a lot in bowhunting in September. But if you can stay out of sight where they can't recognize what you are, you can stop them in their tracks even in November, December and January," Hoppe said.

The cow call, or any call for that matter, is most effective when the caller is hidden. This fact of calling life is especially true for elk, which seem to rely more on their eyes, than any other sense, to verify that danger is near. If a hunter can stay low and make himself more difficult to detect, his cow calls are more likely to do the job in stopping elk.

In light of the cow call's effectiveness, the hunter's tale of woe we started this section with might have had a different ending. It was obvious the bull hadn't seen him. If he had, he would have bolted from the scene immediately rather than waiting a while. The bull had only heard the hunter, and the cow call would have given him the impression that the breaking stick was really just another elk that happened to be near. Most likely, the cow call would have stopped him and presented the hunter with the shot he was waiting for.

The best method for using the cow call to stop elk that either you have spooked or someone else has spooked, is to blow the calf sound in rapid succession. It sounds almost like you're trying to scare the animals. You make two short calls five seconds apart, wait about fifteen seconds, then give two more calf calls. Just keep repeating the sequence until the elk stop or go over the hill.

This sequence has worked on everything from single elk to herds of two-hundred or more. When you have a lot of elk running, you don't necessarily call louder, but you have to call often enough that your sounds finally penetrate the noise that the herd is making as it moves out. When they stop, they'll usually turn and look at you. At this point, if you keep calling, it will verify the sounds the elk were hearing. And it should hold them for a while, even

It is even possible to call an elk back after a hunter has shot at him and missed.
Jim Hamilton photo.

if you do take a shot at them. Often, they'll even stand there after you take several shots, but don't try to press the point with bad shooting. Eventually, they'll figure out what's happening and begin heading out again.

The cow call seems to work for as long as the hunter can remain hidden. As soon as the elk spot you and make a positive identification, even the most potent magic of the cow call won't hold them any longer.

One piece of good news for hunters is that in the period after the rut, the cow call seems to stop bulls better than it does cows. That's not to say it can't stop cows or that it can't stop big herds of elk that include many cows. But the effectiveness of the call in stopping bulls is rapidly becoming legendary.

George Athas, another Gardiner outfitter, was guiding a hunter during the late season once who was having his problems hitting a bull. There were four bulls in the group, but the one the hunter had his eyes on was a big six-point which was just a little more skittish than the rest.

When the hunters jumped the elk, the six-point took off but Athas stopped him with a cow call. The hunter took a shot and missed. Then all the bulls took off. Athas blew his cow call again and all the bulls stopped. And the hunter shot and missed two more times. On his fourth shot, he hit the bull but didn't put it down. As the elk moved out again, Athas called again, stopping the bulls once more. This time, the hunter put the six-point down for good. In all, he had taken five shots at the bull, while the outfitter kept stopping him with the cow call.

Stories of this numbing effect on the sensibilities of bulls go on and on. Bulls are pulled back out of the timber. They're stopped in their tracks. Then there was the one about the hunters from Bozeman and Billings who jumped eight bulls, shot at them, and had them run clear across a canyon.

"They were out there eight-hundred or nine-hundred yards," Athas said. "I kept blowing on the call. They stopped, turned around, and started coming back to us. We brought them back close enough to shoot at them again and kill two bulls. Even when we were dressing out the bulls we killed, the other bulls we called back stayed right there where we could see them. That's just unbelievable. You just don't see things like that."

It's difficult to explain the forces at work, which can make the cow call so effective at stopping and holding bulls that really should know better than to stick around. It boils down to an elk language at work we really don't understand. That combination mew-chirp sound seems to work like a tranquilizer on an elk's mind. It literally defies description. All we know for sure is that when elk hear a rifle hunter make the cow and calf sound and a bull responds to that call, he's as good as dead in his tracks.

Reading the Signs

Too many hunters stumble through the mountains without a clue as to what's going on around them. They look for elk, but miss the messages the bulls and cows leave behind that could tell a hunter where they might be hiding. Hunters listen to the birds and the wind in the trees, but fail to recognize when the elk are talking to them. They see tracks, and droppings, and feeding areas, and can't interpret their meanings.

The toughest part of elk hunting, whether you're calling them in, sitting on stand for them, or stalking them, is finding the elk in the first place. And anyone who hikes the mountains blind is making even a tough hunt much tougher than it should be.

The hunter's greatest ally in his quest to read elk sign is

undoubtedly snow. It leaves an exact record of what the elk are doing and where they go. As a result, the rifle hunter who takes to the mountains in November has a distinct advantage. Snow is a good tool to learn more about elk in a particular area and elk in general.

By getting on a high point and using your binoculars or spotting scope, you can glass over a wide area and tell when there are elk in the country. Their legacy of tracks in fresh snow will show what paths they have followed. Their pawing activity, to reach the grass beneath snow, can be spotted even at a long distance. After the snow has been on the ground for a time, it gets tougher to spot fresh elk activity at a distance. But even then, a close inspection of the tracks will tell the hunter a great deal about whether the country he's hunting is holding any elk.

There are other ways to use the snow, as well. Back when I was young and foolish, and cruising the high country seemed a lot easier than it is today, I learned an awful lot about elk habits by jumping them on purpose, then following them to see where they went. Some people have thought I was crazy for doing hunting that way, but it was almost like a game to me. I'd work my way through the timber, then purposely not shoot a bull the first time I saw him. I'd give him a chance to bolt out of there. Then I'd follow his tracks in the snow and hunt him that way.

Once the elk knows he's being followed, he's a lot tougher to move in on for a shot. It becomes a great challenge. You just stay on his tracks, no matter how tough the going. Those bulls can take you through the worst tangles of deadfall and up the steepest slopes. But if you want to learn the fine details of where elk go and what they do, this hunting technique can teach you a great deal. It's not necessarily the easiest way to learn it, but you can learn.

Vince Yannone, a good friend from Helena, carried the jump-and-track process one step further some years back. When I was working on the book, "A Hunter's Guide to Montana," he told me about an elk hunting experience that few others would even attempt. "I followed an elk one time for four days," he said. "I always pack a sleeping bag, stove, and some food, and I just told myself this was the bull I wanted, so I got a wild hair and kept after him. He was pretty distinctive, a five-by-six that had one brow tine which came down in front of his face.

"I kicked him out of his bed several times, but he always

Snow leaves a visible record of where a bull elk has gone and what he did there. Bob Zellar photo.

managed to stay out in front of me. There was a light snow, though, and I could keep track of him," Yannone continued. "He kept circling within five or six miles of the area where I jumped him and finally, on the fourth day, I headed him off and I caught him out in the open looking down to where I should have been. From where I jumped him, to where I shot him, was about a half-mile. I saw other animals, other bulls, during those four days, but that was the one I wanted."

That kind of hunting attack may seem like folly to a lot of hunters. Frankly, most of us don't get so many chances at bull elk that we're going to be frittering away the opportunities we do get. Most of us just aren't that picky. But if you really want to learn about elk, it's a great way to go. You'll find that elk do basically the same thing time after time. Once you jump an elk in one spot and follow him, you know where they're going to go next because you've been through that routine with them once before.

One thing to remember, however, is that you have to be in

excellent physical shape to hunt a bull that way. But it can be done, and you can literally walk a bull down until you get a shot at him.

Snow can help a hunter in other ways, too. If you can get a good look at their tracks, you may be able to tell whether you're working a bull, cow, or calf. In general, an elk's track is about halfway between those of deer and moose. And often, if you cut a single elk track, it's that of a bull, while a mixture of large and small tracks will indicate it's a cow-calf group which may or may not have a bull with it. A big bull's tracks may give you other clues as well. If the bull has a large, wide, rack, he may have to walk well around trees and avoid tight places between trees. His rack may even leave small scrapes on trees or chips of bark on the ground where his tines touched trees as he he passed. Often, when you're following a group of elk, there seems to be one set that always walks wide around trees and brush. That, very likely, is a bull traveling with a herd.

As you follow the tracks, if you find a place where the elk have urinated in the snow, that, too, can be a sign. A bull will leave a neat, yellow-ringed hole in the snow while the cow's telltale sign appears to be a bit more of a spray. As for droppings, they are tougher to read unless they're very fresh. Come across a steaming pile of elk droppings and you can be sure you're close to what you're after. Other than that, it becomes a game of guesswork with the weather playing a heavy role in their appearance.

One rule of thumb is that, in general, the glossier they are in appearance, the fresher they probably are. Dry, hardened droppings may have been made days, weeks, or even months ago. If the elk droppings are soft and flat and in distinct piles, that probably means they were produced while the animals were still on green grass. Once the elk are on a diet of cured grass and browse, the droppings harden more into pellet form and tend to be scattered over a wider area.

And, finally, the way the tracks are headed can provide still another clue to elk activity. They may wander aimlessly when the animals are feeding, but that changes when the elk are on travel routes. Elk tend to move pretty much in straight, predictable directions. They move through passes, head across slopes, and walk through basins, as if they had a sense of purpose in

By glassing from a high point, you can track elk movements on distant peaks and ridges. Mark Henckel photo.

where they were going. But that changes when the animal is going to bed down. If the elk track suddenly heads uphill and starts wandering back and forth, it's a sure bet that the elk is going to be bedded somewhere up above you. He's laying a trail that he can watch from his bed as danger gets nearer.

It's time then for the hunter to check out the terrain above him. If he spots a small bench, knob, or timber pocket, he should change his track-following strategy. The plan of attack then is to circle around the likely bedding area and come in slowly and carefully from above. That way, he may be able to ambush the bull in his bed, as he watches his back trail.

A bull's penchant for watching his back trail is what makes tracking elk so difficult in the hunting season. They seem to know that they've left signs behind that a hunter can follow. As a result, this circling strategy is a good one to use anytime you think you're getting close to a bull watching his back trail.

Lyn Nielsen, of Deer Lodge, uses this tactic extensively when he jumps elk. If he spooks a bull in the timber, he waits for up to a half-hour, then makes a wide circle around the elk, hoping to spot him as he watches his back trail. Often, the elk have only moved three-hundred or four-hundred yards, perhaps have crossed through some opening, then stopped in the heavy timber on the other side. By sneaking in from above, Nielsen has often spotted the bull watching his back trail, sometimes standing up, sometimes bedded down. It's a hunting method that requires great stealth and patience. It is also aided by a good knowledge of the area you're hunting, so you can tell what's up ahead when you jump a bull.

The important thing in this, or any elk hunting situation, is to keep a sharp mind and open your senses to the signs the elk leave for you. You have to be able to spot them, both the ones that are near to you, and the ones you catch through your binoculars. And, once you see them, you have to be able to interpret what you see. Even the small signs that elk leave behind can make a difference in your strategy, tell you whether you're on the right or wrong track, and determine whether your tag is full or empty once the hunting season is done.

Stand Or Stalk

Some rifle hunters were blessed with lead in their rear ends and ice water in their veins. Others are fountains of energy, unable to sit for more than five minutes at a stretch, yet somehow able to put mile after mile behind their long strides. For hunters like these, the decision to stand or stalk is easy. Let the stump-sitter do just that, freezing with a drip on the end of his nose. And let the long walker cover his ground.

Most of us, however, fall somewhere in between those two extremes. We have to make conscious decisions about the plan

Hunters working slowly through the timber may sneak up on a bedded bull.
Jim Hamilton photo.

of attack we choose during the rifle season. And in order to make those decisions, we should weigh the odds of success.

Outfitters often work the best of both worlds. When they have groups of clients to spread through the mountains of elk country, some stand and some stalk. The outfitters know their hunting country well enough that they can position some hunters on stand in likely escape and travel routes. The other hunters then hit the timber and hunt there with the knowledge that they might take a bull themselves or could move elk into the sights of those on stand.

Hunting on stand can also be an effective technique in any situation where there are apt to be many hunters in elk country. In some opening-day situations, for example, it seems like there are orange-clad hunters behind every tree. With that many hunters about, stalking becomes almost impossible. If there is snow on the ground, a hunter can begin following a set of tracks only to find that another hunter cuts in ahead of him and starts doing the same thing. You can sneak into the bedding areas only to find several other hunters doing the same thing.

At times like that, a hunter should use those other moving bodies to his benefit. Let them push the elk to you, rather than you pushing the elk to them. If you have scouted the country you're hunting in or have the benefit of years of experience there, a hunter should know the escape and travel routes. Perhaps there's a low saddle between drainages that the elk move through. Maybe there's a finger of timber that joins two large forested areas. Or, perhaps there's a certain mountain face that the elk move across. A hunter could do much worse than to plant himself in one of these places and plan his ambush. Make yourself comfortable. Get yourself a steady rest for your rifle. Then wait for the elk to come to you. Stump-sitting like this may not seem to offer much excitement for the hunter used to covering a lot of ground, but it puts a lot of elk meat in the freezer every year.

If you have a little more elbow room in the places you hunt, there are other options available in terms of hunting strategy. The first thing a rifle hunter has to determine is what stage of the season he's working. If the snow is piled deep on the mountaintops, the elk are going to be lower on the slopes. If it's early enough that the high country is still relatively open, the best option is to go high for them.

My own personal favorite is to hunt the heads of the drainages early in the season. The majority of the elk will be well back in the mountains at that time of year. In the early mornings and evenings, I can work the big open parks and small meadows. During the rest of the day, I concentrate my efforts in the timber.

That timber hunting is the secret of success for many elk hunters. For others, it's a nemesis they avoid at all costs. Perhaps it's because we live in an age of flat-shooting, high-powered rifles which allow a hunter to reach out and sting a bull at long distances. Perhaps it's our basic dislike of being anyplace where we feel closed in and can't see long distances. Or perhaps, it's the fact that the shots a hunter gets in the timber tend to be quicker and the terrain more cluttered than in the open parks. But whatever the reason, too many hunters try to wander the open ridge tops and walk the open parks all day long. In the process, they miss the fact that elk are definitely a timber animal during most daylight hours.

For some hunters, this disdain for timber is a matter of past experiences with elk. Every time they head into the dark forest, they seem to spook elk out ahead of them. And once they spook, the hunters feel they're gone forever. The judicious use of a cow call can stop some of those fleeing elk. And another way to work them is to literally run after them. You might be surprised by the fact that if you do run after them, you can often catch up to them and get a shot as they head through a clearing or hold up to find what's chasing them.

Even if you do spook your share of elk at the start, the experience and stealth you gain from your days in the timber, will help you become a better timber hunter. Eventually, you will get the hang of it. And in time, you'll learn that the majority of the hunters that are successful year in, and year out, are the ones who know how to work in the timber.

Almost without exception, these successful hunters' timber-hunting strategy includes working slowly, carefully and quietly. They wear quiet clothing like wool or fleece that won't make a lot of noise when it brushes against twigs and trees. Their boot soles are soft and supple enough to muffle movements. And though they have to wear blaze orange in most states to stay legal, they avoid wearing large blocks of it. If you can break up the big blocks of orange, it will make it more difficult for the elk to spot you.

And despite the fact you can't see very far ahead of you, binoculars are a real asset in the timber hunting. They force hunters to concentrate their vision on smaller areas. You can pick out the pieces of elk that way, which you might miss without them. Perhaps all you can see is a leg, an ear, or an antler in the distance. But that is enough to let you know there are elk in the area and allows you to plot your stalk from there.

If I were to plan my perfect hunting day, it would be to follow the patterns that the elk establish in their own day. For many of them, that means starting the day low in their feeding areas. I'd work my way up the mountains during the morning. I'd search out the timber in the early afternoon. Then I'd follow the finger ridges back down in the evening in hopes of finding a bull moving out into the open parks to feed.

Calling to the Gun ■

If you spot your animals well in the first place, the hunt itself may be short.
Ron Shade photo.

This strategy would take several things into account for the mid-season rifle hunter. For one thing, it would put him in places at the right time for elk to be there. But even more importantly, it would allow him to work several levels of elevation in the same day. Too often, hunters commit themselves to a single plan of attack. Perhaps they decide to work the high meadows and the elk turn out being low. Maybe they work low and the elk are high. And most hunters seem to forget the middle of the mountain, which may be the best place of all under most conditions.

All of these hunting strategies take into account that you don't know exactly where the elk are in the first place. There's one other situation we should talk about and that's spotting your elk first, then going after him. This is something of a mixture of standing and stalking which might be the easiest way to hunt of all during the rifle season.

Doug Laubach had a tag to fill in rifle season a few years back and we turned this scouting strategy into a good bull for him. I had filled my tag already that year but had been doing some glassing, just to see where the elk were hiding. In the process, I had spotted three bulls that were coming out and feeding right at dark in a particular open park. They had been in the same spot for two evenings when Laubach and I decided to go after them.

We had their history figured out and knew it would be late in the evening. We got above them and after they fed out into the open park, we peeked over the edge and Laubach got his six-point bull. It was just that easy.

Observation time was at least as important as the actual hunting time in filling his tag. After the two evenings of observation time, the hunt itself lasted just one hour. And if you think it was a fluke and that observation time isn't as important as hunting time, be advised that we worked another six-point bull the same way the following year.

The hunter has to plan his stand-or-stalk attack depending on the conditions at the time and the state of the hunting world around him. If he's got a group of hunters to work with, or it seems that every other elk hunter in the world has congregated in his hunting spot, or the elk are on the move themselves, then a stand can be the most effective way to go. It offers the footsore, lead-rear-ended, or out-of-shape hunter an alternative as well. If you like to cruise the mountains and search out new places, or if there aren't enough other hunters to move the elk, then it's time to stalk the open parks and timber at the right time of day to find the elk there. It's an individual decision that each hunter must make every time he heads into elk country. And it's a decision that a hunter must weigh well, if he hopes to find success.

Map Work

Okay, so you goofed. Your best buddy gave you explicit directions to a great elk spot he hunted a few years ago. But instead of ending up in a remote high country meadow, you're looking at a paved parking lot, complete with visitor center, picnic tables, and a viewing platform to watch the activities at a new mine site for pet rocks.

Something happened between the time your friend went hunting and you arrived there. Civilization came to the back country. Man came in and changed things around. And, in the process, another good elk hunting spot went the way of development.

While this example may sound far-fetched, those types of things happen in one form or another every year to elk hunters. Even the remote reaches of elk country undergo changes from time to time. They aren't always as radical as our example, of course. But they can be just as devastating, if you're all dressed up for hunting and find you have no place to hunt.

Hunters who scratched and scraped their way over a four-wheel-drive trail to reach good elk hunting, might be upset to find the state came in and paved the road, opening it up to everything on wheels. It can be just as bad to pin your hopes on a spot, only to find out that a seasonal road closure keeps you ten miles short of your old elk camp. And it wouldn't help much to arrive at elk camp only to find the whole area had been clear-cut.

The way to prevent these kinds of surprises is to do a little map work before the season, especially if it's been a few years since the last time you hunted that spot.

"There's nothing worse than planning to go to a roadless area, and once you get there, you find there are roads all over and you could drive through it," said Ralph Saunders, a Billings hunter who turned map-maker after he nearly lost his life while on a trip to pack out a bighorn sheep. Saunders, his brother Bruce, and friend Bill Johnston, got caught on a high-mountain plateau at night

If you study maps closely, you can often identify the places elk will be hiding. Jim Hamilton photo.

during a November blizzard. They knew the plateau well, but even with a map and compass, they were lucky to escape with only minor frostbite. The incident helped Saunders make his final decision to produce good trail maps of the mountains of southern Montana. And since then, his faith has been renewed when it comes to the worth of a good map.

"Maps are valuable to me before and during an elk hunting trip," he said. "There are different kinds of maps that will tell people different kinds of things."

National Forest or Bureau of Land Management maps will show land ownership and roads. Forest Travel Plan maps show which roads are open, closed, or have seasonal or vehicle restrictions on them. Those maps are available through the particular national forest headquarters or state BLM offices.

Finally, there are the series of 15 and 7½-minute U.S. Geological Survey topographic maps, which are the basic bibles of the backpackers and hunters who head into the high country. These show forested and open areas, the rise and fall in elevation, water courses, and man-made features such as roads, houses, and mines. For the Rockies, these maps, and information about them, are available by writing to: Western Distribution Branch, U.S.

Geological Survey, Box 25286 Federal Center, Denver, Colo. 80225.

"A person has to spend some time with these maps. They need to take some time to learn them," he said. "If you study those maps and really take a look at them, you can also learn some things about the country that can help in finding elk. If you can read the contour lines and forested area, you can find the open, wind-swept areas, the timber pockets, the head basins, and you can even see the travel routes that elk will take from one drainage to another. It might even give you an idea of the habitat type by the terrain."

Hunters should use the maps for other purposes as well. They can help a great deal in locating likely elk hunting spots, making your hunting as versatile as possible, and positioning your camp site.

For my own part, I like to look for places where the heads of several creek drainages come together and put in my camp near there. That way, I can work those creek drainages until I find the elk. Too often, hunters commit themselves to a single drainage simply because of the placement of their camp. Once they're committed, they may find there are no elk in that drainage, leaving them with many miles of mountains to travel to search out other areas. Then, when they locate the elk, they may have to move camp to get within easier striking distance of them.

A different kind of camp problem comes about when hunters set up too close to their hunting area. This way, their camp activities spook the elk out of the area. Once spooked, the elk may go many miles into another drainage, effectively putting them out of reach of hunters working out of that camp.

This penchant for elk to move long distances and be concentrated in certain drainages, while absent in others, is a fact of hunting life known well by the outfitters. It's a fairly common practice in some parts of elk country, for example, for outfitters who find their own areas devoid of elk, to move into distant drainages and fire their rifles in bedding areas there, in hopes of spooking the herds back to where they're more easily reached by hunters from their camps.

After the rifle seasons are well underway, it's also not uncommon for elk to search out remote hideaways. These are the pockets that hunters rarely reach. Perhaps that's because they're far off the beaten path. It might be that their topography is so rough that travel there is difficult. Or it could be that they're close enough to the beaten path, but they're simply overlooked in their search for other hunting spots.

Map work is vital to finding these hideaways. A hunter can locate them much more quickly with a topographic map than by walking miles and miles of mountainous country each day.

In fact, it's almost a nightly ritual in many elk camps to haul out the maps and plan the next day's hunt. By using the maps, groups of hunters who haven't found elk yet can plot a strategy to cover different areas in hopes of locating them. Drives can be planned on the maps as well. Or, if you're like Saunders, you can find out things that worked in other years.

"I mark my maps up with all sorts of things," he said. "I have no respect for them at all. They're there to use. I write on them, mark them up, put kill locations on them. I put notes on them as to how far it is from spot to spot and how long it took to get from one place to another. It really helps when you want to remember what happened a few years back, and it gives you ideas of what you should be doing now." Maps are also invaluable if you do happen to knock down an elk and have to leave it there. Elk country is big country indeed, when it comes down to finding a particular spot where you left an elk. And missing the exact spot by a couple of hundred yards when you go back, can mean that you never find that elk again.

"You need a compass, and by making two sightings off it and using the map, you can pinpoint the spot pretty well," Saunders said. "You don't need a real expensive compass to do it. You shouldn't have to pay over $15 for a good compass.

"For the hunters who are a little more serious about it, they might think about buying an altimeter, too," he added. "After correcting the settings at known elevations, you can tell just about the exact elevation where you left the elk. Between that and the compass sightings, you should be able to find it easily. A temperature-compensating altimeter costs between $135 and $175. It can really help to find wallows again or an elk you had to leave back in the timber."

A set of maps, compass, and an altimeter will tell a hunter a great deal about where he's been and where he's going in the mountains. They can help in locating likely places where elk will be hiding, as well. They won't replace thorough scouting, however.

Calling to the Gun ■

Using maps to make your hunting successful works well in all seasons.
Don Laubach photo.

There's nothing as effective as hiking an area and getting to know it on an intimate basis through personal observation.

But don't overlook the map work, either. Maps can be a life-saver if you happen to get lost, or are simply turned around in foggy or snowy weather. They can give you new insights when you get back to camp and have run out of places to look for elk. And I have yet to meet a hunter who can read maps, that hasn't learned a new thing or two about even a very familiar area by looking at them and studying them in the off-season.

As a hunting tool, they are invaluable in elk country in many ways. And besides, as Saunders put it, "There's no reason for people to skimp on maps. If you go elk hunting, you know you're going to have to spend some money. By the time you're done, the map expense is going to be the least of it."

On The Move Again

Good things come to those who wait, or so the old saying goes. For elk hunters, that good thing is the annual migration down from the high country. It's a phenomenon of late November and

December, encompassing the final days of elk season and the weeks thereafter.

Some hunters actually wait for it, holding off with their elk trips until the snows grow deep in the high country and the temperature dips below zero. If you don't have a camp in the high country, the horses to get you there, or the strong legs and back to carry you and your gear far back into the mountains, this season will bring the elk to you.

Some hunters feel that deep snows are all that is needed to push the elk out of the high country. That, in fact, is only part of the equation that puts elk on the move. Elk actually are equipped to deal with heavy snow quite well. They're very much at home on steep slopes where the snows have difficulty piling up very deep. They can paw their way down to the grass that lies below. And their pawing motion dislodges snow which, in turn, dislodges other snow as it rolls downhill.

Crusted snow is another matter. Two inches of crusted snow will move far more elk than two feet of the fluffy variety. In part, that may be because the crusted snow is more difficult to paw through. But, I've also been told that a heavy crust can irritate or even cut the elk's feet, further urging them on the migration path.

The final piece of the puzzle is cold temperatures. Although an elk's fur is thick and heavy enough to withstand the coldest temperatures the Rockies can throw at them, the temperature dipping below zero seems to be the last ingredient necessary. A good cold snap combined with deep snow and crust is like a magnet for pulling elk out of the high country.

All that adds up to some tough conditions for hunters to get around in, too, of course. If the hunters had to work the snow, the crust, and the bitter temperatures far in the backcountry, most of them would probably pass on the migration as a good hunting time. But this is the time when the elk are available without long hikes. It's a time when the elk may be within easy walking distance of the road. They'll be within easy dragging distance, too. And for the hunter without the benefit of horses to pack an elk out, those are important considerations.

Adding to the hunter's fondness for the migration is the fact that bulls often seem to be the first ones to make a move. In country with plenty of elk, it's not uncommon to see big bull bunches,

The combination of snow and cold moves elk toward their traditional winter ranges. Michael Sample photo.

numbering fifty or more individuals, move within reach of waiting hunters in late November. There have been some frighteningly high elk kills under those circumstances, when herds get caught between groups of hunters. Yet it's not really something that can be regulated for or against with any degree of accuracy. It only happens when weather helps the hunters too much and makes the elk too available to them.

Another thing about the migration that hunters like is that it's a moveable feast over a period of several weeks or even months, if the weather is mild. If you can locate a migration path, there may be new elk herds moving along it every day over the last few weeks of the season. If no good bulls show up today, they may arrive tomorrow. And if not then, perhaps they'll be in sight the next day. A hunter who persistently works the migration paths will eventually be rewarded in most years.

One rule of thumb for the hunter who likes to hunt the migration is that new movements will be triggered by each November storm. But a hunter doesn't need to be there on the day of the storm to take advantage of the situation. The first clear day after the storm is soon enough. And, sometimes, the second day after the storm is even better. By hunting that second day, it gives the elk time to react to the storm and a day to move into the area.

The migration routes themselves are traditional pathways for the elk. For the most part, they don't change from year to year. It's been part of the elk's lives to move along these paths each year with the coming of winter. Cows pass that tradition along to their calves which, in turn, pass it along to calves of their own. Older bulls pass it along to their understudies in the bull bunches, who also pass it along to younger bulls in future years, when they too will become dominant.

Bull groups and cow groups may choose different paths to the winter range and, in fact, they may even choose different winter ranges. What you have to understand here is that elk tradition is strong and is something that comes about over time. It's the survival strategy which has worked for these animals and kept their genes alive in the population over centuries. The animals whose survival strategies didn't work, have died out over those same centuries. That's why some elk may migrate many miles to reach a particular winter range, even when other winter ranges might be closer.

Calling to the Gun ∎

If you can identify the migration route, the elk will be somewhere along that path. Ron Shade photo.

This ingrained tradition is what carries the elk over the same paths every year. But that doesn't mean it never can change. A clear cut in an area that was previously covered with dense timber, altered the migration path in one spot I know of. A late elk season, to take advantage of animals migrating out of a closed area in January and February, has also changed their migratory traditions.

While it won't hold true in all situations, the simplest way to find a migration route is to know where the elk summer, and where there's a wintering ground located. Then draw a straight line in between the two areas. Somewhere along that line will be a long ridgetop, a mountainside that runs for several miles, or a creek drainage that connects those two areas. That migration route may stretch for many miles. It may go through vast acreages of dense timber, around several mountains, or through several drainages. And the elk themselves may be scattered in small bunches all along that route between the summer and winter areas. Over the last weeks of November, all a hunter can count on is that somewhere along that path, he will find elk.

The snow conditions of the migration also give the hunter one key as to where the elk will be found. Because snow piles deeper on flat ground, the elk will tend to feed on the side slopes. They won't be in the creek bottoms or on the high flats when the snow is measured in feet rather than inches.

But it is a fact that bulls seem to be able to tolerate deeper snows and may hold at higher elevations once they reach the winter range. Maybe it's because the cows have shorter-legged calves to think about which can't tolerate deeper snow. Maybe that's why the cow and calf groups move to the lowest parts of the winter range. Or, perhaps it's the same phenomenon at work as in the summer, when the cows and calves pick out the choicest parts of the summer range, while the bulls are left with the inferior areas.

Whatever the reasons for the migration paths, the choice of feeding areas, or the winter ranges where the elk migration ends, the truth of the matter is that the migration can be a good time to ambush a big bull. The old herd bulls which were much too far into the backcountry for most hunters to reach in the rut, suddenly are coming out to you. The old herd bulls which found a hiding place so far removed from the mainstream during the post-rut period to be bothered by anyone, are now within dragging distance of your car or truck.

If you've got the patience to wait that long, or simply have gone through the earlier periods of the season without filling your elk tag, the migration offers you one last good chance at taking a bull. Hunting the migration, may mean you'll have some snow and cold weather to contend with. But if the bulls are willing to travel so many miles down out of the high country to meet you, the least you can do is walk a short distance into elk country yourself, and give them a one-gun salute.

■

END OF THE TRAIL

All good things come to an end, even elk hunting. For some, that end comes in the blast of a rifle or the twang of a bowstring. An elk crumbles and falls, there is a time of elation, and then the work begins in packing the elk out. For others, there is the dread closing day of the season. No elk has fallen, but the guns must be put away for another year nevertheless.

The end of the trail seems to be a melancholy time for most hunters. It is, after all, an end rather than a beginning. The bright promise of opening day is long gone. The crisp mornings, warm afternoons, and cool evenings spent in the glory of elk country, must be put behind.

But there is still work to do and concerns to be addressed by the elk hunter. For the successful, there is a carcass to be prepared for the trip out of the mountains. If you want good eating for the winter ahead, that means careful consideration of how you handle the meat. It means taking precautions to keep birds, bears, and coyotes at bay. And it means learning skills about getting the animal out of the mountains, whether by horse, backpack, toboggan, or simply dragging it down a trail.

The end of the trail concerns itself with other things, too. There are young hunters embarking on their first elk hunting trips that should be considered. And there are the old-timers among us, who have seen the mountains age, the elk herds shrink or grow, and who may be walking these trails for the last time in their lives.

As for the elk, they, too, are reaching an end. The warm months of lush grass, the rutting season of autumn, and the big migrations ahead of deep snows are just a memory now. There are the harsh realities of life and death on the winter range. These are the survivors which must face the hard times if they hope to see the spring sun shine again.

And for elk hunters, the time for planning next season has already arrived. If they hope to better their chances for success in the season ahead, it takes a year-long dedication to detail. There is elk talk to be practiced. Books to be read. Maps to be studied. And scouting to be done. If the hunter only learns enough about the elk and the hunting that lies ahead of him, there will be happy days in the season to come, when he reaches the end of the trail.

Once They're Down

After the echoes of the rifle shot die out in the high country, the real work begins. First-time elk hunters have no idea just how much work that can be. If all you're accustomed to is white-tailed deer, mule deer, or antelope, the prospects of field dressing, then dragging or packing out an elk can be frightening indeed.

You see the five-hundred to eight-hundred-pound carcass lying before you. You feel the elation. Then you look in your hunting pack. If you don't find such things as rope, a very sharp knife, and a saw or ax in there, you're off to the wrong start already. If the weather is warm and you don't have mesh game bags, cotton sheets, or cheesecloth, chalk up another demerit. And then there are such items as flagging material or toilet paper that can be a big help, too, if you find them there.

Obviously, you need a sharp knife to field dress the animal. But be prepared to have it go dull on you. Elk hair will take an edge off a blade quickly. If you're alone, rope can be invaluable to help stretch the forelegs of the animal so you can be in a position to work on it. I was caught short once and field dressed a good bull while it was lying on its side on a steep slope. It can be done.

If you've prepared the animal well, pulling them out with a horse is relatively easy. Mark Henckel photo.

But it isn't any fun. The game saw or ax comes into play to split the brisket, pelvis, and backbone, if you plan to quarter the elk. Even the most versatile hunting knives just weren't made for such work. And finally, there are the game bags, sheets, or cheesecloth needed by the early-season hunter. These keep the flies from laying their eggs on the meat while still allowing the meat to cool.

Cooling out a big animal like an elk is always a problem, even in cold weather. If you don't open the throat and take out the wind-pipe, for example, it could trap heat and sour the neck area around it. If you don't skin out the massive shoulders in warm weather, the elk could go bone sour. And if you don't get it up off the ground so the air can get underneath it, the backstraps can spoil. You might be surprised to find out elk can even spoil in the snow. Between the insulating properties of the snow itself and the heavy fur of an elk, it can hold heat inside for a long time.

Cooling out an animal quickly, whether it's an elk, deer, or antelope, will insure good eating when you get its meat to the dinner table. That translates into getting good air circulation all around the carcass. Ideally, it means getting the elk quarters hung up off the ground. But many of us aren't equipped for that with just the things found in our hunting packs. The next best thing

End of the Trail ■

is to get it off the ground by propping sticks or logs underneath it.

If you have to leave your elk in the mountains for a few hours or a day to get horses or some help to get it out of there, you should take some additional precautions. Birds, bears, and coyotes have learned to home in on kill sites to pick over the gutpiles. And they certainly know what to do when they find an elk carcass there. If you have to leave the animal there overnight, you can expect to at least have the birds find it. In fact, watching and listening for birds is one way to find the spot where wounded animals have fallen or, if you can't find a carcass on the return trip, where you left the animal.

Another method of finding the elk again is to mark a trail back in to the site. Many hunters carry commercial flagging material like the highway crews use when they're working on a road. These tough plastic strips are usually brightly-colored and provide an easy trail to follow. All you have to remember is to remove the flagging when you're done with it. If you don't have commercial flagging material, toilet paper will work just about as well. The only problem here is that if it snows overnight, you'll find that your flagging blends in pretty well. And wet, heavy snow may pull it down off the branches.

One other consideration, if you have to leave your elk in the mountains for a time, is to provide some protection for the carcass before you leave. Cut pine boughs and branches and pile them deep on top of the elk. The branches will allow air to circulate around the elk, but will help discourage birds from making a meal out of your freshly-tagged animal. It may take a little more time to protect the elk that way, but it could save a lot of meat. When a big flock of birds begins attracting other birds, it doesn't take long to strip a hind quarter.

For coyotes and bears, it's best to leave as much human scent in the vicinity as possible. That means urinating all around the area. It may mean hanging some sweat-soaked garments on nearby bushes. Put anything there that you think might smell strongly of human odor. It just might make the difference between the elk becoming your dinner or one for the coyote or bear.

Bears, in fact, are pretty much a fact of life that hunters must think about whenever they get into elk country. Black bears are scattered over most of the elk range in the Northern Rockies. In my particular hunting spots, there are grizzly bears to be concerned with as well. But before you chalk up the bear talk to simple scare tactics, rest assured they are a worry which is very real.

Rod Churchwell, Frank Rigler, and I were supposed to head back toward Churchwell's kill site to bring the elk out. Almost as an afterthought, Rigler decided to bring along a freshly-sighted-in, new 300 caliber rifle along. We were on horseback headed for the elk at about noon on the day after the kill.

Tired of riding, I finally decided to walk and lead my horse. We were only about two hundred yards from elk with me in the lead. And frankly, I scarcely thought about bears as I glanced toward the elk, spotted the place where we left him, and then walked with my head down. It wasn't until I was thirty-five yards of the elk that I looked up and surveyed the scene a little closer. There, lying flat on the elk, was a black bear which appeared ready to defend its meal.

I told Rigler that I had a bear tag in my pocket, that he should pass me his rifle, and that we'd reclaim ownership of the elk right there. I took him square between the eyes. It wasn't much of a hunt, and the prospect of filling my bear tag that way didn't excite me too much either. But it was about the only way we were going to get that elk back without risking our own good health.

In a way, it was fortunate that the incident did involve a black bear, rather than a grizzly. Not that black bears are any less able to cause trouble. But, grizzlies are more unpredictable, especially when guarding a kill or den site. And once you've seen the extent of their power, it does command your respect.

Another hunting friend, Gene McCoy, was searching out a narrow gulch which sometimes holds elk during the early part of the rifle season. As he worked one of the washes, he came upon a set of elk antlers which was sticking up out of a pile of leaves and dirt. Upon looking further, he found that the whole elk was buried there with only its antlers showing.

As near as he could piece the chain of events together that led to that bull's demise, it was the end result of a grizzly kill. The bear had taken the elk, then stashed it beneath the pile of debris the way grizzlies often do. It was enough to give McCoy an eerie feeling, wondering where the grizzly might be right now.

But the more he got to thinking about the elk antlers that were sticking out of the ground, the more he began to wonder about the size of that rack. It wasn't a spike or brush bull. In fact, it

End of the Trail ■

The grizzly-killed elk that Gene McCoy found had a huge set of antlers.
Don Laubach photo.

was obviously a herd bull, one of the tough guys of the elk world, which had fallen prey to the bear. It was big enough that he decided to go back the next day with a saw and cut off the antlers.

He checked the area out carefully and didn't see any signs that the grizzly had been back. So he cut off the antlers and brought them back to town. To give you an idea of the size of the elk that bear brought down, the antlers green-scored at 392 ten years ago when he cut them off. And even now, ten years later, the antlers still weigh twenty-six pounds. That the grizzly could take down an animal like that while it was in its prime, makes a hunter think twice about charging right in on a kill site.

In the end, everything you do after your elk is on the ground becomes part of a single journey. It's one made up of steps that should be measured, slowly and carefully. Only if you take care of your downed elk properly in the first place, then exercise some caution when you return to pack it out, can you reap the benefits of good meat, good times, and good health, once your hunting is done.

Getting Them Out

Remember these words of wisdom the next time you drop into a bottomless canyon, hunt the jungles of deadfall, or plan to hike in twenty miles from the trailhead to do your elk hunting. As spoken by many a veteran of elk country, they are: "If you plan to shoot a bull back there, you'd better plan to take along a loaf of bread and a Zippo lighter. That's because you're going to have to cook him and eat him on the spot."

The first time I heard those words, I laughed. Pretty funny stuff. Pack some bread and a Zippo. Eat him on the spot. Then I learned about elk country and packing elk out of it. And I understood the deep, dark truths of what had been told. There are indeed some places that you just don't want to shoot an elk. These spots hold elk every year. But even if you do get one down there, you're literally not going to be able to get them out of there. At least, you're not going to get them out without killing yourself or a horse.

The ability to move an elk from the kill site back to your vehicle is, or should be, a viable concern for elk hunters. When you're talking about moving an animal that large over the long distances involved in the mountains, you have to be able to assess the methods available to you, as well as the type of terrain you have to cover. And no matter how willing the candidate, even the strongest hunters among us can't drag an elk uphill forever.

Basically, hunters fall into two groups when it comes to getting their elk out of the mountains. One group has horses. The other group has not.

Going the horse route is undoubtedly the easiest on the hunter. If he can avoid the high country rodeos, where pack horses kick, and buck, and take off for parts unknown, it's a great way to go. You can ride a horse of your own, or walk the pack horse with a lead rope, and pack a lot of elk in a painless fashion.

The simplest way to load a horse is to have a Decker saddle and panniers. Just slip an elk quarter in each pannier, cinch them up, and you're ready to go.

If you don't have a pack saddle, it's possible to pack an elk out, a half at a time, on a regular saddle. First, you cut the elk in half between the second and third ribs. Then, take an ax and split the length of the backbone without cutting the hide. Finally, you take your knife and skin each half back two to four inches. The elk

A half-hitch around the elk's muzzle makes it easier to drag them out by horse.
Mark Henckel photo.

half, at this point, is ready to throw over the saddle with the backbone up and the legs pointing toward the back of the horse. After you get the load balanced, you slice the hide you skinned back just enough to force it over the saddle horn. To finish off your load, take the stirrups and tie them up to the saddle horn. Then tie the elk off to the cinch ring on each side so it can't flop around. Packed this way, half an elk rides amazingly well.

This same system works well to carry out halves with a sawbuck pack saddle. The only difference is that you slice the hide in the front and back and force them over the sawbuck.

If there is snow on the ground and there aren't too many tight spots to negotiate, most hunters have their horse drag the elk where they need it to go. The first thing required if you want to drag a bull is to stabilize the animal. That's accomplished by tying one of its front legs onto one side of its rack with a short piece of rope. This holds the head upright and keeps the antlers from catching in the snow. Then you take a long rope, tie it around the neck, and put a half-hitch around the muzzle of the elk so that you have a straight pull on it. Then put two wraps of the other end of the rope around your saddle horn and start your horse in the direction you want him to go. Just make sure you don't try to tie that rope off to the saddle horn. You want to be able to get rid of that rope if your horse decides he doesn't want any part of it, or if the elk starts getting away from you.

There are other ways to pack elk out with horses as well. There are many wild times in the mountains associated with that packing, too. Suffice it to say, there's an art to horse packing that most of us don't have. Outfitters seem to have it, but it seems many have developed a whole new vocabulary to go along with it.

So if you have a choice of using horses or not using horses, use them. But it's best to leave the horse packing to the experts, whether that expert happens to be an outfitter or someone who has done it many times before. For most of us working stiffs, horses aren't a consideration anyway. Most of us don't own horses. And if we borrowed them, we wouldn't know what to do with them. So we drag them out by hand, pack them out on our backs, or, if we're lucky, balance our elk, a quarter at a time, on a motorbike and slowly take them out of the mountains that way.

Most hunters who go into the high country figure that if they get an elk down far from their vehicles, they're going to pack them out on their backs. Be prepared for the fact that it's a tough way to go. You're moving an awful lot of weight, sometimes over long distances. And it's not just tough on your back. It can hit you hardest in the ankles and knees.

Hunters who pack elk out on their backs have two options available to them. One is to bring the animal out in quarters, roughly dividing the elk into four even pieces. That's accomplished by splitting the length of the spine, then cutting the halves between the second and third ribs. The advantage of this method is that the bones, and the hide if you wish, will hold the quarter together. The drawback is that you have to carry the weight of the bones, too. If you opt for bone-in packing, just be sure to lash the quarters to your packframe with cotton rope, rather than nylon which will stretch and loosen under the weight of the elk. The other way to go is, to bone out the animal, pack the meat into sacks, and then load the sacks into your backpack. This eliminates the weight of the hide and the bones and lightens the overall load. But you have to be very sure that the meat is cooled out well before you pack it out this way. Put warm meat into a backpack and it may spoil before you ever get out of the mountains.

Other hunters simply drag their elk out. If there's snow on the ground and someone has pulled out an elk ahead of you, this can be the easiest way to get your animal to your vehicle. After those drag trails have thawed and then frozen again, it can be almost like a bobsled track if the snow is deep enough. When the going is easy like that, one man can move an elk. If the going gets tough and a good drag trail isn't avaiable, it may be two men on a quarter to get the job done.

A relatively recent variation on an old theme is the advent of the kids' toboggans. Curt Collins, a Billings hunter, can remember his boyhood days in Colorado when his father often took a full-size toboggan into the mountains to pull out the deer or elk he took there. The toboggan simply made it easier to move the animal, distributing the weight better, and avoiding the friction of hair going over snow. This system still works well, but buying a full-sized toboggan just for elk hauling these days, is anything but cheap. Instead, kids' toboggans are available on sale for $10 or less in most areas. Some are molded into a toboggan shape that will easily handle a big elk quarter or small half. Others are just a rolled-up sheet of pliable plastic with a hole so you can get a

Once the first elk starts a drag trail, the rest of them follow along easily. Ron Shade photo.

hand grip on them. If you want to improve on the design, just install some grommets near the edge so you can lash the big quarter or small half in place. They reduce the friction involved to the point that some hunters even use them when dragging elk over grassy slopes, to make the pulling a little easier.

I've accomplished much the same thing with nothing more than a big sheet of heavy black plastic. We put the elk on the plastic and used that to pull the elk, just lashing it in with a piece of rope. The arrangement pulled well, but the plastic eventually tore and tattered when it was pulled over trees and rocks.

If most of these methods sound like a lot of work, there are good reasons for this. Most of them are a lot of work. You simply can't move anything which is that heavy, over the long distances involved in the mountains, without burning a lot of calories and straining some muscles along the way.

The best advice is to be in good shape yourself before you attempt to pack an elk out of the mountains. Try to get someone to help you, if you can. And if there's any doubt in your mind at all about whether or not you can get the job done, hire someone like an outfitter to get the elk out for you. Who knows, if you do it that way, you may end up with more than just your elk at your

End of the Trail ■

vehicle. If things go like they usually do when you deal with beings of the equine persuasion, you might even learn some new vocabulary terms from the outfitter and end up knowing how to talk to horses yourself.

Old And Young

Perhaps, a section like this has no place in a book called Elk Talk. Perhaps, it's the perfect place.

So far, we've concentrated our talk on elk in all seasons. We've taken them from the calving grounds to the summer range. We've courted their affections during the rut and we've chased them in the post-rut period from the high country clear down to the winter range.

We've talked about what to wear, how to call, where to look, and why you should be doing all those things. But we've really talked very little about the different types of people who hunt for elk. So far, we've pretty much taken for granted that we're talking about your average elk hunter. He's a person who is in good enough shape to hike the mountains day after day. He's skilled enough in woodcraft that he can get himself out of any trouble that might befall him. In short, he's an experienced hunter in the prime his life, whose skills and physical ability are well-tuned to life in the mountains.

The problem with that assumption, is that it really doesn't encompass a wide enough range of individuals. Not every elk hunter is put together that way. It totally ignores the youngsters, those teenagers who are just getting their feet wet in the elk hunting world. And it also fails to address our older hunters, the pioneers at the game, who may have hit their prime some years ago but still look to their days in the mountains each fall with a great deal of anticipation.

Each group deserves their due. And each also deserves the respect, courtesy, and unselfish assistance of every other hunter in the mountains, whether we're talking about deer hunting, duck hunting, or elk hunting.

For the young, the time we spend with them in the mountains, and the things we teach them there, will establish patterns that they follow for the rest of their lives. The love and respect for elk that we impart to the young are at least as important as the

Passing on the traditions from old to young is just part of life in the mountains. Ron Shade photo.

ways and means to hunt them. In the process, we also have to teach them how to survive in what can be a harsh world in the mountains.

To do your best with the young, you have to prepare them for the worst as well as the best of hunting situtations. That aspect of hunting life was hammered home hard, when my eldest boy reached an age when he was old enough to begin going after elk. He had been taught about life in the mountains and what to do when things went sour. And all that paid off one evening during archery season.

It was in his freshman year of high school, and we had walked into the mountains in the dark that morning. We kept to the high ground all day, working the likely elk spots. And when evening arrived, it was time to hike back out. Our plans were to split up and work our way down a ridge and meet at the bottom. By the time we got down off the mountain, there would be just enough light left to get to our vehicle for the ride home.

But somewhere along that ridge, my boy got off into some timber and hit the wrong ridge. He wandered off into another drainage, then got caught in a deadfall jungle as darkness settled into the mountains.

End of the Trail

He had his fanny pack along with him which included the basic necessities of flashlight, toilet paper, rope, some candy bars, matches, and other miscellaneous items in case he got lost. And he followed my directions explicitly for what to do when you get lost and darkness settles in. He found himself a spot to spend the night, built himself a fire, cut some pine boughs for a bed, and planned to wait until daylight. By having him stay in one spot, it prevented an injury that could easily take place by stumbling through the mountains in the dark. And it also put him in one spot for the search party, rather than having the searchers trying to track down a moving target.

For my part, I waited at the vehicle for him until 10 p.m. before heading back to town and rounding up some friends for a search party. It was almost midnight when we made it back to the mountains and fanned out in pairs to look for him.

I started up the drainage looking for him, and eventaully found him at about 3 a.m. up on a little bench about two hundred yards above the creek. His first comments were predictable, repeated often by someone who's lost and then found, "What took you so long?"

It was a valuable lesson for him, and for my other children who were to join me in elk country in the years that followed. And it underscored the importance of preparing the young well for their hunting trips before you set foot in the mountains. It's not enough to simply tell them how to hunt. You have to teach them how to survive as well. And you have to give them the tools of survival and instruct them in how to use them before the hunt begins.

With older hunters, the problems often take a different form. These hunters possess the knowledge of the mountains. They have the years of experience behind them. But all too often, they lack the compassion of their peers when it comes to heading out on what may be the final elk hunts of their lives.

Where's the glory, for example, in racing past a pair of older hunters on the trail to beat them to a prime hunting area? How much would be lost if you passed up a morning of hunting to help someone a little older in years pack their bull out of the mountains? And what about all the grandfathers, fathers, uncles, and friends who you never think to ask whether they'd like to come along on this year's hunting trip?

My favorite story about helping an older hunter took place far

All other hunters deserve our assistance and respect, no matter what their age. Don Laubach photo.

away from elk country and involved a deer hunting situation. An older hunter had knocked down a whitetail and hung his tag on the animal about the time a school bus was passing by, taking kids to school in a nearby town. The bus driver pulled over, climbed the hill, helped the man drag the deer to the road, and got it situated on his vehicle before climbing back into the bus and continuing his journey. Had the kids gotten to school late, the time still couldn't have been better spent.

Not every older hunter needs that kind of help, of course. In one recent elk season, I had the pleasure of hunting with Glenn Saunders, of Columbus, on opening day in the Snowcrest Range. Saunders was seventy-years-old at the time and we climbed a brutally-steep slope in the early-morning darkness to reach our stands. But at least, he had the decency to wait for me to catch my breath many times during that climb. And his tales of elk and deer hunts of decades gone by, made the trip one that I'll always treasure.

Too often, in our rush to hunt and hunt hard, we forget the others that are out there doing the same thing. It becomes almost a competitive undertaking to see who can get a bull, who can get the biggest bull, and who will be the winner.

Hunting was never meant to be that way. It's a time for kindness and caring, both to the people we meet while hunting and to the elk themselves. And no one deserves it more than the old and young hunters among us. They are our future and our past, a living legacy of our times in elk country.

Together For The Winter

The winds blow harsh and cold when winter settles into the Northern Rockies. The high country is empty now, except for the pine squirrels, martens, and blue grouse still trying to scratch out a living. The echoes of elk bugles that filled its September mornings have long since died out. The orange-clad forms of rifle hunters who walked its open parks and stalked its timber, have long since packed their guns away. And even the scattered herds of elk which were strung out along its trails during the migration, have forsaken the high country for the easier life of the winter range.

While the high country is buried by deep snows and feels the chill of winter winds, the low country is alive with elk. On well-defined winter ranges, the survivors of the hunting seasons are facing yet another battle for life. Death on the winter range doesn't come with the razor-like incision of an arrow, the quick shock of a rifle bullet, or even the vicious attack of a grizzly bear. There are more insidious factors at work here. Death is a lingering menace, fueled by the deep snow and cold, aided by parasites and disease, and made final by numbers of elk, amount of food, and length of winter.

In some years, winter can be devastating on an elk herd. Harsh conditions, in fact, have killed elk by the thousands in Yellowstone National Park. There is no more sickening sight than to look around you and see eight, huge, mature bulls lying dead in a space no bigger than your living room. It's just as bad to watch a cow seemingly at rest in the snow have her head droop lower, and lower, until she can't hold it up any longer in her weakened condition. And then there are the calves which fall prey to coyotes or, in some parts of the Rockies, wolves, when they can't keep up with the herd.

Unfortunately, the big bulls are often the ones hit the hardest by tough winters. After the rigors of the rut, there isn't much time for them to regain weight lost chasing and breeding cows. Of all elk, they go onto the winter range in the worst condition. Along with calves, these big bulls are the least likely to survive, when the going gets tough. Combine this mortality with the hunter harvest and it's easy to understand why the truly big bulls are such a treasure.

Surveys done on winter ranges in the Gravelly and Snowcrest Mountain Ranges of Montana, for example, show just how rare those big bulls can be once the hunting seasons are done. Extensive aerial and ground surveys have found that branch-antlered bulls make up only one or two percent of the total elk numbers found there. Spike bulls, which are protected in some of the hunting districts that feed the winter ranges, make up about an additional ten percent of the herd.

Certainly, that bull ratio will vary from winter range to winter range, but it does point out how much they're in the minority. And it also points out just how much pressure is being exerted on bulls, both naturally and through man-made causes.

The mortality factors that can get to elk are numerous. Deep and crusted snow may keep them from getting to feed. Drought years may wipe out the grasses they feed on. Scabies and infestations of ticks may rob them of their vitality. And there are always those predators around, waiting to score on the old and infirm.

While not wanting to add to that stress, the winter range is a good opportunity for hunters to get to know elk a little better.

End of the Trail ■

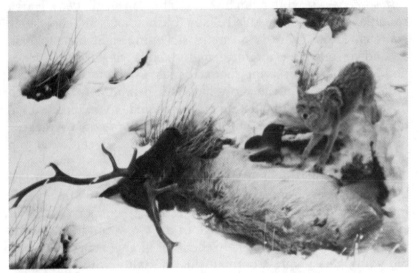

Winter exacts a heavy toll on the elk world that only benefits the scavengers. Ron Shade photo.

Because they're concentrated at lower elevations, the elk are readily accessible to people who want to get out and see them.

What you're likely to witness is the true communal nature of the animals. They're more concentrated than at any other time of the year. They're more vocal, too. No one knows what they're talking about, of course. Perhaps it's how tough or easy the winter has been. But it's a fact that if you really want to hear cow talk, calf talk, and bull talk, you can get an earful on the winter range.

It was some years back when Rod Churchwell and I donned our cross-country skis for a moonlit journey onto the winter range. The moon was full that night, as we set out across Deckard Flat, and we could see quite a distance considering it was midnight when we began.

Out on the flat, there was a herd of eight-hundred elk. And we skied right toward them. Between the white clothing we were wearing and the glow of the moon, the elk didn't seem to pick us out right away. As for the elk, they were chattering and talking back and forth. That elk talk only increased the closer we got.

We skied right into the middle of one group and cut them in two before they spooked. A herd of about two-hundred headed off in one direction while the other six-hundred began running

Elk gather in large herds on the winter range where they wait for the spring to arrive. Ron Shade photo.

the other way toward their timbered bedding ground. All was fine for a time, until the herd of two-hundred decided they should join the others. These elk came back at a dead run, heading right for us. I finally got down behind a rock for safety's sake. It was the closest I ever came to being caught in an elk stampede. Churchwell was about a hundred yards away and he, too, avoided getting trampled.

It was a unique experience that brought out all the herd tendencies of elk on the winter range. They talk. They gather in big herds. Their social interaction includes sparring matches among the bulls. And when two cows get angry, they rear up on their hind legs and punch at one another with their front hooves.

If the winter is mild enough, you can see them feeding on the windblown or south-facing open slopes. If it's tough, you can find them pawing for grass buried beneath the snow.

It's a difficult time for them, at least as difficult as the rigors of the hunting season. And, frankly, some of them won't survive it. But for the hunters who truly love the elk of the bow and rifle season, the winter range is something they really should see. You can learn from the elk here about how they live, how they talk, and how they get along with each other. And you can grow to appreciate them, too, for all they must endure to earn the warm summer sun and the crisp mornings of autumn.

End of the Trail ■

All too often, an elk hunter is stopped by knowing too little about the bull of his dreams. Ron Shade photo.

Planning For Next Season

I have a friend who lives his elk season every day of the year. In Art Hobart, of Billings, there is one dyed-in-the-wool elk hunting fanatic.

If the archery season is on, you'll find him dressed in camouflage, somewhere in elk country, trying to sneak in on a bugling bull. When the gun season arrives, he'll change his dress to hunter orange, go to the high country, and buck the deep snows to get in position for a migration period ambush. And when all his weeks of elk hunting are over, he anxiously begins counting the days until the next season arrives. Hobart makes cow talk and bull talk in the off-season. He searches out maps to study. He scouts new country and reacquaints himself with familiar places. He reads everything he can get his hands on about elk. And he works at building the year-long frenzy that breaks loose once again when opening day of elk season arrives.

There are certainly more successful elk hunters among us. Hobart doesn't get his bull every year. But it's not for lack of trying. And to me, he epitomizes the image of the hunter who gets as much fun out of his preparation, as he does out of his time in the field.

Planning for next season should be fun. And it should last all year long. There are many things to do, depending on how you plan to hunt.

If you're going to hunt within driving distance in your own state, plan to put in plenty of scouting time during the off-season. Even in spring, the rubs and wallows of last fall can be located and marked on a map. Search out the hiding places, the little pockets where bulls will hide when pressured by hunters. And get to know more country than you ever hope to hunt.

Vince Yannone, of Helena, learned his hunting country on an intimate basis by hiking it after work. He'd race home from the office, grab a sandwich or two, then hike until dark. These summer jaunts helped him learn an entire mountain range and almost all the spots within it where elk would hide.

If you're not hunting an area nearby, you have your choice of either traveling there to scout it out before the season or, perhaps, hiring an outfitter who does know it well. But be sure the outfitter you hire is a good one. You can obtain lists of licensed outfitters from most state wildlife agencies in the Rockies. If not, try the state outfitter associations. Then do more than just pick your outfitter at random.

Contact the outfitter well in advance and find out things like the length of his hunts, the price, and what type of country he hunts. Is it a pack-in situation into the backcountry or does your outfitter specialize in day trips out of a hunting lodge? Does he charge extra for things like shuttles to and from airports, trophy handling or rifle scabbards and saddlebags? How many hunters are there per guide? And can the outfitter provide you with a cross-section of references, such as past clients or local businessmen who can attest to his claims.

Elk hunters should understand that they generally get what they pay for in an outfitter. Fees from $2,000 to $3,000 for a ten-day hunt are charged through much of elk country, and that doesn't include the license. Some outfitter fees run higher and some lower. But just remember that if your outfitter comes cheap, the quality of the hunt may turn out that way, too. The more information you get, the better the chances you'll end up with the kind of hunt you want.

One thing the outfitter can do for you is advise you on how to get a non-resident elk license. In many elk states, the number of non-resident licenses is limited. If you decide not to use an outfitter, write well in advance to the state wildlife agency and request license information and application forms. A full year in advance isn't too soon to get your information, either.

Once you make your decision on a place to hunt, bury yourself in literature about that area. While elk are elk, there may be local tendencies that could spell the difference between success and failure. If detailed maps are available, get them. If guide books have been written, buy them. And if you can get a lead on specific individuals that hunt that area, try your best to get in contact with them.

Any information you can assimilate during the off-season is going to make you a better hunter once the season arrives. It won't necessarily replace scouting trips, but it can help give you a jump on the situation, if time is tight and your ability to get to the area is limited.

The off-season is also a good time to practice your calling techniques. Buy a cow call and bull call and blow on them. If your

If you only have enough imagination, you'll see your bull in your dreams all year long. Mark Henckel photo.

wife objects, stash them in the car. If your budget allows it, buy one set for the car and one for your home. In the past, hunters pretty much had to rely on their memories to get the sounds right on those calls. But these days, there are audio and video cassettes on the market to jog your memory or introduce new sounds. For the hunter who plans to call in his elk, the off-season is the best chance he has to learn as much as he can about the ins and outs of elk talk. If he waits until the season arrives to do his learning, he'll blow more chances and scare more elk than if he just kept quiet.

And, finally, get yourself in shape for the hunting season ahead. Elk, for the most part, are not creatures of the flat and open spaces. Their habitat is the mountains where steep slopes and oxygen-sapping conditions are the rule. Asked to describe what elk hunting was like, I once told a friend that it was simply long, long, long periods of up, separated by too short periods of down.

The hunter who gets himself in shape for the mountains is going to be doing himself a favor when the elk season arrives. If he can hit the trail and go for miles, he stands a much better chance of finding an elk. If he can do it with ease, he also stands a much better chance of making it home without a heart attack to contend with in the backcountry.

In short, a hunter should do all the things in the off-season that he can to prepare himself for the hunt. The better prepared he is for opening day, the better his chances of getting an elk. And the better his odds for having fun both in and out of season, as he lives his year hunting elk or thinking about hunting elk.

It's a common misconception in elk country that to bag a bull takes ninety-nine percent luck. That is pure bunk. The more successful the elk hunter, the more likely it is that he has removed as many variables as he possibly could. That hunter has cleared all the hurdles which stood between him and success and continues to clear them every time a new season dawns on elk country.

The consistently successful elk hunter knows about elk. He knows about his elk country, too. And, more and more these days, he finds his success by speaking the language of elk talk.

■

Other books available from E.L.K., Inc.

The Elk Hunter
The Ultimate Source Book on Elk and Elk Hunting from Past to Present, for the Beginner and Expert Alike

Deer Talk
Your Guide to Finding, Calling, and Hunting Mule Deer and Whitetails, with Rifle, Bow, or Camera

Elk Tactics
Advanced Strategy for Hunting and Calling Elk

The Coyote Hunter
A complete guide to tactics, equipment and techniques for hunting North America's perfect predator

Short in the Saddle
True tales of the outdoors and the funny things that happen along the trail.

For product information, orders, or free catalog, call toll-free E.L.K., Inc. 1-800-272-4355. Visa and MasterCard accepted. Web site: www.elkinc.com Email: info@elkinc.com P.O. Box 85, Gardiner, MT 59030